WISCONSIN ROAD GUIDE TO MYSTERIOUS CREATURES

THE WISCONSIN ROAD GUIDE TO MYSTERIOUS CREATURES

By Chad Lewis

© 2011 On The Road Publications

All rights reserved. No part of this publication may be reproduced or transmitted in any form or by any means, electrical or mechanical, including photocopy, recording, or any information storage or retrieval system, without the permission in writing from the publisher.

ISBN: 987-0-9824314-2-9

Proudly printed in the United States by Documation

On The Road Publications
3204 Venus Ave
Eau Claire, WI 54703
www.ontheroadpublications.com
chadlewis44@hotmail.com

Cover Design:	Kevin Lee Nelson
Illustrations – Cases – 10, 16, 18, 19, 21	Johnny Sixgun
Cases – 1, 2, 3, 7, 11, 20, 26	Kevin Lee Nelson
Cases – 14, 15	Terry Fisk

DEDICATION

This guide is dedicated to my son Leo Lewis, the most unique creature of them all!

TABLE OF CONTENTS

Preface i

Acknowledgments iii

Foreword v

Introduction ix

Case 1 – The Vengeful Witch of Witch Road 1

Case 2 – Blackie – The Shadow Being of Caryville 8

Case 3 – The Shadow Demon of Nekoosa 15

Case 4 – Jenny, the Sea Serpent of Lake Geneva 20

Case 5 – Pepie of Lake Pepin 29

Case 6 – The Monster in Devil's Lake 36

Case 7 – Bozho – The Lake Mendota Sea Serpent 44

Case 8 – The Lake Monona Sea Serpent 52

Case 9 – Lake Ripley's Serpent 58

Case 10 – Red Cedar Lake Monster 65

Case 11 – Phantom Chickens of Chicken Alley 72

Case 12 – Aliens Bring Pancakes 78

Case 13 – Alien Abduction in Bloomer 86

Case 14 – Mysterious Beast of Eau Claire 95

Case 15 – The Hellhounds of Meridean 101

Case 16 – The Bear-Wolf Beast of Holy Hill............................108

Case 17 – The Beast of Bray Road...115

Case 18 –The Gnomes of the Devil's Punchbowl.....................121

Case 19 – The Rock Tossing Gnomes of Holy Cross Road......127

Case 20 – The Huldrefolk of Washington Island 132

Case 21 – The Pig Men of Brussels..139

Case 22 – The Cumberland Beast...144

Case 23- The Bigfoot of Granton..150

Case 24- The Bigfoot of Danbury...160

Case 25 – Blue Hills Bigfoot 165

Case 26 – The Mineral Point Vampire 171

PREFACE

Report Your Experiences – This guide is set up for you to have an adventure. I recommend that all legend trippers bring along at least a camera and journal to document your findings.

Private Property – Unfortunately a couple of the locations listed in this book are on private property. Please respect the privacy of the owners and only view these places from the road. If you do venture onto private property please make sure that you have prior permission, otherwise you may end up with a hefty trespassing ticket to go along with your creature sighting.

Safety – Many of these cases come with a side dish of danger. Not only do you have to watch out for the appearance of these mysterious creatures, you also have to keep a keen eye out for other known dangerous animals. Keep in mind that many of these locations are out in the middle of nowhere, so always try to have someone with you in case of injuries and emergencies. At the very least make sure that you tell someone where you are going so if you don't return, we will at least know where to retrieve your mauled remains.

Accuracy – I have made every effort to ensure this guide is current and accurate yet some errors will inevitably surface. If you find better directions, take better photos, or manage to capture one of these beasts please contact me so I can make the changes for future editions of this book.

Roadside Attractions – This guide is just the tip of the iceberg of your adventure. Getting to these locations is half the fun, and Wisconsin is filled with so many oddities that you should never

WISCONSIN ROAD GUIDE TO MYSTERIOUS CREATURES

run out of places to explore. Allot some time to hit all of the odd roadside attractions that you will bump into along your adventure.

Outside the Norm – Veteran legend trippers know that the best adventures come by getting out of your daily routine. Travel the back roads, spend the night at the dodgy roadside motel, and grab a meal at the old mom and pop diner. Trust me the chain businesses will not miss you.

Acknowledgements

First and foremost I have to thank all of the witnesses (both living and deceased) who shared their remarkable stories for the rest of us to enjoy, including: Joe Simonton, Steve Krueger, Dennis Murphy, James Hughes, Billy Dunn, and Brent Lorbtske.

This guide would not have been as complete without the aid and assistance of the dozens of librarians, researchers, and historians, who kindly lent their expertise and provided me with a wealth of information. A big thank you once again goes out to Sarah Szymanski for all of her work making this a better guide. I also want to thank my wife, Nisa Giaquinto, for all of her sage like advice.

Thank you to Johnny Sixgun and Kevin Nelson for the wonderful illustrations that really cause the creatures to leap from the page.

I must give a giant thanks to all of my fellow researchers (both past and present) whose wonderful material added much to this guide, including Charles Brown, Linda Godfrey, Craig Lang, Richard Hendricks, Jay Rath, and Todd Roll.

Since this book is all about adventure I have to give a huge thank you to the world's greatest legend trippers, Noah Voss, Kevin Nelson, and Sean Bindley. Of course I cannot leave out all of my friends at *Wisconsin Today*.

Finally a huge debt of gratitude goes out to my Unexplained Research colleague, Terry Fisk, whose research and investigations can be found throughout this entire guide.

WISCONSIN ROAD GUIDE TO MYSTERIOUS CREATURES

Foreword

"Wisconsin...A country where the only sounds are the cries of owls, the whippoorwills, and the eerie loons at night, and the wind's voice in the trees, and – but is it always the wind's voice in the trees? And who can say whether the snapped twig is the sign of an animal passing – or of something more, some other creature beyond man's ken?

-- August Derleth "The Dweller in Darkness"

We've all seen the movies, watched the shows, and heard the stories. You know the ones I'm talking about—the ones where everyday people have strange encounters with something truly inexplicable. It may happen while driving down a deserted lane late at night, other times while hiking or camping in a remote wilderness area. It could be a brief sighting of something tall and hairy at the edge of a wood—too bear-like to be a wolf, too wolf-like to be a bear, and far too *human* looking for comfort. Or occasionally one might stumble upon a rare and special place deep in a glen...a place where the 'spirit roads' meet. In places like these one might catch a glimpse of something they thought was only a folktale or urban legend. These are what I consider Wisconsin's greatest *un*-natural resources. Sure, we occasionally hear similar tales nationwide, but what makes this state unique is this: in Wisconsin bizarre encounters happen *daily*.

Is this the "Dairy State" or the "*Scary* state"?

Does that make Wisconsin stranger than other states? You bet it does. Wisconsin is a real oddity. It's a place where our mundane world can unexpectedly veer off, taking us down a detour into realms of myth and legend. That signpost up ahead—your next stop—doesn't read "Twilight Zone;" it states something far more suggestive. It reads, "*Welcome to Wisconsin.*"

WISCONSIN ROAD GUIDE TO MYSTERIOUS CREATURES

You saw something you swear wasn't a "normal" animal? Join the club!

Wisconsin's forests are larger, darker, and full of primal mystery; the marshlands and bogs are places for spectral encounters; creatures could lurk just beneath the surface of our deep and secluded lakes; and without having to stretch one's imagination, hidden glens could easily be the home to fairies and gnomes. That's because in Wisconsin we have an unusually rich and unique heritage stemming from both indigenous beliefs and diverse immigrant folklore. Wisconsin's syncretic mixture of mythologies includes legends of phantoms, beasts, extraterrestrials, and other strange phenomena that can't even be categorized. After considering all this and after having lived here for most of my life, I've come to believe that Wisconsin is to America what Transylvania is to Europe—that is, a liminal space or borderland betwixt our world and others far stranger, a haunting (or haunt*ed*?) land saturated in dark legends and enchanting folklore. As Wisconsin author August Derleth puts it, in Wisconsin "…there persists an intangible aura of the sinister, a kind of ominous oppression of the spirit quickly manifests to even the most casual traveler."

The House on the Rock, an imposing and eccentric abode perched high atop a rocky crag, is our "Castle Dracula." *Dr. Evermore's Forevertron Sculpture Garden* in Sauk County, filled with colossal and mystifying scrap metal creations, is our answer to "Dr. Frankenstein's laboratory."

Like Transylvania, Wisconsin has become a favored setting for horror and fantasy novels. Why is it that famous authors of said genres, such as Stephen King, Neil Gaiman, and Peter Straub, have chosen Wisconsin as the backdrop for some of their recent titles? Not that this is anything new…Milwaukee native Robert

FOREWORD

Bloch wrote his famous novel PSYCHO in 1959, inspired by the gruesome murders committed by Ed Gein in Plainfield, WI a few years prior.

You might be wondering, "Where do these cryptozoological creatures come from?" Well, your guess is as good as mine, but I'd wager that many of them have been here a very long time. The Native Americans tell tales of creatures like the Wendigo, Water-Panthers, Thunderbirds, Bear-Walkers, and hairy ape-like creatures very similar to what we call "Bigfoot" today. Perhaps other creatures arrived as stowaways in the collective consciousness of immigrants, just waiting for a chance to manifest themselves in a new land, enriching our eerie ecology: trolls from the Scandinavians, gnomes from the English, vampires from Slavs, the Po N'Zhong from the Hmong, werewolves from the French, and even the dreaded 'chupacabra' or 'goat-sucker' from the Hispanic community. They've all created a beachhead within the state's cultural identity and are here to stay.

We all know the world is getting smaller. Farmland is quickly being converted into subdivisions; pristine natural areas are being crisscrossed with a grid work of new roads and high-voltage power lines. Perhaps Wisconsin is the last refuge for things-that-go-bump-in-the-night, a sanctuary for the sinister, and a preserve for the paranormal.

Looking for a supernatural safari? If so, this book will be your trusted guide.

I've known Chad for over a decade. Over the years we've explored and investigated every corner of our mysterious state. Be it a remote forest, hidden cave, cursed stretch of road, or the local historical society—if there's a legend to be found, Chad will find it. The bestiary you have in your hands is your best chance of being one of the lucky few who have glimpsed something that isn't supposed to exist. Just as with other uncommon flora and fauna, whether a black bear, a Blue Heron, or a rare lady slipper orchid, if you want to see it in the wild, you first need to know where it lives. This book will show you how to spot the hidden habitats of Wisconsin's most exotic creatures.

Do you think you're ready?

Considering that you're reading this book, chances are you're already one of those adventurous types who aren't content to read about others' experiences from the safety of a comfy recliner; you want a chance to witness something firsthand. So don't just settle for armchair cryptourism, get out in the field and witness something incredible with your own two eyes. Remember…a GPS won't help you map out the state's psychogeography. Instead, let this road guide be your dowsing rod, as it will certainly point you in the right direction. Perhaps your experiences will become the next chapter in Wisconsin's ever-growing folkloric heritage. If there's anything I can guarantee about Wisconsin, when traveling its back roads you're bound to find *something* weird. So grab your camera, flashlight, mojo-bag, wolfs bane, garlic, and some brave friends (one always needs bait); it's time to hit the road.

Kevin Nelson

(Artist, Folklorist and Adventurer)

Midwinter 2011

Introduction

As children we all fear the hideous monsters dwelling under our beds and those demonic creatures that inhabit our closets patiently waiting for an opportunity to catch us with our guard down. As we become adults we quickly realize how irrational our childhood fears were and become thoroughly convinced that mysterious creatures only exist in Hollywood. Yet as you are about to discover, Hollywood's best creatures are simply no match for the amazing variety of unknown beasts roaming around Wisconsin.

Cancel your travel plans to Transylvania, postpone that adventure to Loch Ness, and forgot about having to venture out east to Salem, because this guide will show you that Wisconsin has more bizarre creatures than nearly anywhere else in the world. And that is where this guide comes into play. Filled with directions, warnings, folklore, creature history, and witness drawings, this guide all but begs you to get out and explore these places for yourself. As you start your adventure through Wisconsin you will have the opportunity to encounter some of the world's best known creatures like Bigfoot and deadly sea serpents. However, as you pass through the dark back roads you also may find yourself staring down more obscure beasts like pig men or phantom chickens.

Regardless of what creatures you encounter you better be certain that your pre-adventure bravery stands up to the challenge. Many seasoned legend trippers have lost out on photographic or video evidence as they were inextricably frozen with fear while the mysterious creature retreated back into the shadows. This guide will help prepare you so you do not suffer their same fate.

One final piece of advice is to make sure that you bring along some friends to add to the adventure and to also help corroborate your story. Plus this way you never have to outrun these creatures, you'll only have to outrun your friends.

Keep an eye out,

Chad Lewis

CASE 1 – THE VENGEFUL WITCH OF WITCH ROAD

The Vengeful Witch of Witch Road

Where To Encounter It:
Callen Road (Witch Road)
Ripon, WI

Directions:

From Ripon, go south on Highway 44/49, turn left on Cty Rd. KK and follow it for 1.9 miles and then turn right on Callen (Witch) Road. The old witch's house will be on your left side.

What is left of the home is on private property—Please view it from the road

Creature Lore:

In days of old, being a Witch was not the wisest of career choices. Faced with a life of being feared, misunderstood, ostracized, imprisoned, or even sentenced to a brutal death wasn't too appealing. Witches historically have been viewed as social outcasts, practicing the dark art of witchcraft while closely aligning themselves with the Devil. There is much debate in folklore over the actual physical makeup of a witch. Are they normal rational men and women whose earth-based rituals and spells are simply misunderstood, or are they some type of unknown cryptozoological creatures?

The extent of the strength and power of these witchcraft practitioners varies widely throughout folklore. Thought to possess supernatural powers, witches were able to inflect great physical, mental, and spiritual harm to those who fell under their wrath. The work of witchcraft was routinely blamed for poor harvests, loss of livestock, and even the disappearance of small children. Today the popular perception of a traditional witch is that of a hideous old woman whose pitch black clothing is matched only by her heart. Yet this wasn't always the case…one of the many powers of witches is their ability to shape shift and transform themselves into many different forms. They often would operate under guise of animals or morph into a young attractive girl in order to achieve their unholy objectives.

History of Lore:

One of the most fascinating legends in Wisconsin revolves around an old decrepit house that continues to hide its hideous secrets. According to legend, nearly seven decades ago a mysterious old lady lived all alone in a small home on the lonely outskirts of Rosendale. Those who were brave enough to venture out to the area were treated to the chilling sounds of bizarre chanting emanating

CASE 1 – THE VENGEFUL WITCH OF WITCH ROAD

from the home. Rumors soon began spreading that the woman was deeply engaged in unholy rituals that were cursing the land. The woman's reputation as a witch rapidly spread, causing more and more curious onlookers to visit the area. Sticks, rocks, and other miscellaneous objects were routinely thrown at the home in attempt to aggravate the witch. Eventually, even the dark arts could not keep the witch alive, but before her death she used her power to put a curse on the home and the surrounding land.

Investigation Log:

For those who visit the short secluded stretch of Callen Road, the sensation that it is inhabited by a witch seems to set in immediately. The heavily wooded area starts to slowly squeeze in as the trees along the road creep together to form a dark canopy where not even the light can escape. The trees seem to manifest the uneasy feel that the road conjures up. The twisted

The vengeful witch of Witch Road

and knotted braches morph into frightening shapes and appear to come alive as you pass by. The whole area looks like it remains frozen in a painful pose from a time long since passed. It is out here that one of Wisconsin's darker legends rests. Most people travel to the site with the hope of encountering the witch, but they often find that the old witch is only the beginning of their troubles.

For years the area has been plagued by strange balls of light that float along the road. These will-o-wisp lights dart back and forth between the road and the trees as though controlled by some unseen force. One witness told me that she finally got the courage to walk the road at night by herself, but as she was walking she noticed a small ball of white light in the woods that was moving parallel to her. She noted that the light seemed to mimic her every move, even gaining speed as she began jogging up the road. Over the years I have received dozens of similar reports detailing a light that routinely changes its color, shape, and size.

As I previously mentioned, the rural area is bordered with creepy looking trees. My first visit to Witch Road came during a bright day when the sun was beaming down, yet as soon as I rounded the bend in the road the place took on an almost impossible darkness as the bizarre shaped trees all but extinguished the sun. In this atmosphere the trees seem to take on a life of their own. Legend states that one such tree in front of the house stands out from the rest because of its uncanny resemblance to that of a witch. You may struggle to find the exact tree, as no one is sure which one it is, although I get plenty of people who tell me they stared down the menacing witch tree.

In 2007, I filmed a segment with the Discovery Channel's *A Haunting* program that featured a bizarre event that occurred on Witch Road. A couple and their young son arrived out at Witch Road just as the sun was losing its grip on the day. After locating the old house, the husband thought he heard voices coming from the home, although the family was certain they were the only living people out there. Not ones to let their imagination get the better of them, the family brushed off the unidentified voices and began walking about the place, soaking in the weirdness. Then, their normally very shy son yelled out "hello" as his gaze was fixated on

CASE 1 – THE VENGEFUL WITCH OF WITCH ROAD

the woods in front of him, yet his parents could see no one there. Using her son as a sort of psychic barometer, the woman began snapping several photos when she saw a shadow from the corner of her eye. Turning to get a better look at the shadow, the woman noticed that once again, no one was there. With the odd events piling up, the couple continued on their investigation, passing by the house once again. This time the husband found himself overcome with nausea as he stood near the run-down building. He quickly moved and discovered that the sick feeling dissipated, leaving him with the feeling that he had stepped into some type of cursed spot. Convinced that something strange was lurking out at Witch Road, the family headed home only to discover that several of their photos that coincided with the strange action were blurred, while the rest of the photos were perfectly fine.

Eerie feelings of "something not quite right" are par for the course out at Witch Road. One woman was checking out the area during the safety of the daylight, when about halfway down the road she experienced a "very strange sensation" when the road became "noticeably darker and felt...well...weird." A gentleman reported that one night he took his wife and a friend out to the road. They were positioned on the road, looking at the run-down house, when the air was pierced by a "very audible scream" that shot out from the woods. Looking around for possible sources, the group was certain that they were alone. On yet another occasion, a woman and her mom were driving through Callen Road. They just passed the curve and the old home when she looked into her rearview mirror and saw a huge black form on the side of the road.

WISCONSIN ROAD GUIDE TO MYSTERIOUS CREATURES

Deserted house where the witch was said to live.

The area is also home to the spirit of a mischievous little girl who playfully interacts with visitors. People often see the ghostly image of the girl shyly peek out from behind a tree, only to hear her giggling a few seconds later from the complete opposite direction. Who or what this young girl is remains unknown. It is possible that she had some connection to the land or even to the witch? Perhaps the little girl is not really a girl at all and instead is one of the many guises taken on by the witch.

Technically, there have been very limited accounts of anyone actually seeing the witch even though most accounts blame the weird noises/screams, uneasy feelings, and the ghostly girl on the presence of the witch. Throughout history, if a woman of a certain age decided not to marry, move out into the country, and live a life alone, she immediately became the town's token witch. I have found no evidence that any witch ever lived out on Callen Road, yet

CASE 1 – THE VENGEFUL WITCH OF WITCH ROAD

I haven't disproved it either. The actual history of the home remains mostly unknown. One of our Unexplained Research message board users wrote about the history, claiming that the house was once occupied by two unmarried sisters who had inherited the farmland from their parents. The sisters took on some hired hands to maintain the farming, and being that they were very self-sufficient, they rarely made trips into town. Of course, this independence sparked many rumors among the townsfolk, and the legend of the witch began. Upon the death of the sisters, the house sat vacant for quite some time. Since then, the home has been repeatedly battered by vandals, arsons, and Mother Nature.

So the question still remains…Did/does a witch live out on Callen Road? In the end, the best way to find out if the mysteries of Witch Road are true is to visit the area for yourself and come to your own conclusion. But be warned…just because the old house looks abandoned from the road, many swear that it is by no means empty.

WISCONSIN ROAD GUIDE TO MYSTERIOUS CREATURES

Blackie – The Shadow Being of Caryville

Where to Encounter It:

Old School House Area
Caryville, WI
Building is on Private Property – Please View From Road

Directions:

From Clairemont Ave. in Eau Claire, take County Road E to the west. Turn left on County Road H and follow it until 930th Ave. where you will turn right. The schoolhouse will be on your left.

CASE 2 – BLACKIE – THE SHADOW BEING OF CARYVILLE

Creature Lore:

Relatively little is known of the mysterious entities known as shadow people or shadow beings. What is known is that, whatever these beings are, they often appear in a somewhat humanoid form, although they lack any noticeable facial features or expressions. True to their name, many who see them initially think that they are nothing more than a passing shadow caught out of the corner of their eyes. It is thought that these creatures somehow lurk only in our peripheral vision, disappearing from sight when viewed directly. Although their ultimate purpose remains hidden, widespread speculation has branded them with a sinister agenda, some going so far as to classify them as demons.

History of Lore:

It is safe to say that the field of study around shadow people has netted more questions than answers. One of the more compelling unknowns in shadow people research is the question of just how long these creatures have been interacting with humans. The category of creatures known as shadow people became internationally-known during the 1990s, after being featured on several episodes of Art Bell's widely popular *Coast to Coast A.M.* radio program.

In 2001, researcher Heidi Hollis wrote *The Secret War*, one of the first books dealing with shadow people. The book included Heidi's own experiences with the unknown creatures. Since the publication of *The Secret War*, numerous shadow people books have been published.

Up until the 1990s, the rural community of Caryville was all but forgotten by nearly everyone but its own residents. It was in the '90s that the eerie legends of the place began to widely circulate. Terry Fisk and I have tried unsuccessfully to uncover the origin of the stories and were unable to locate any documentation of them prior to the '90s. One version of events tells of two young friends who were engrossed in an intense Oujda board session at one of Caryville's cemeteries, when one of the girls became "possessed" by one of the spirits with which they were communicating. The young girl began to flop and writher on the ground as she spoke in unknown tongues. Help was called, but the girl was beyond reasoning with and had to be taken from the area in an ambulance. Up until recently, the townsfolk of Caryville took great strides in trying to keep out curious sight-seekers by continuingly asserting that nothing strange was going on in Caryville. The constant denial only fueled the talk of a conspiracy, and soon word starting spreading that the town must be hiding something.

Today, the people that own the church and schoolhouse have adopted a more open house policy. They hope that by explaining the real history and heritage of the area, they can dramatically decrease the amount of visitors, thereby eliminating the vandalism that has plagued the area.

Investigation Log:

The old school house of Caryville is an immensely popular destination for those looking to come face to face with the supernatural. Every year I get dozens of reports from curious sight-seekers from around the Midwest who have trekked to this secluded little town, determined to experience its many mysteries. The list of supernatural legends attached to the area around the eerie-looking old school house is very impressive. It would not be difficult to devote an entire book to the folklore surrounding the bizarre activity taking place at Caryville. Although this is a guide to mysterious creatures, I would be remiss if I didn't arm you with at least a brief synopsis of all the other phenomena you might come face to face with while out at Caryville.

CASE 2 – BLACKIE – THE SHADOW BEING OF CARYVILLE

The most widely-told legend is of a young boy who, long ago, was looking to escape the wrath of his abusive father and decided to seek sanctuary in the safety of the school house. Unfortunately, the boy chose the wrong Wisconsin evening to find refuge, as the subzero temperatures froze the boy as he shivered in his desk. The tragic death caused his spirit to continue haunting the place where he met his fate. Legend states that anyone brave enough to sit in the cursed desk will feel the presence of his spirit. Over the years, I have spoken with several witnesses who claim that upon sitting in the desk they lost all control over their body and were physically unable to remove themselves from the desk without the aid of friends. By all accounts, the witnesses felt as though some unseen spirit or force was trying to keep them from getting up and thereby exiting the school house. The old school is on private property, which means that surely no one would go inside, but if they did, they would see that the place has many old school desks inside; which desk is the cursed one is undetermined. In our book, *The Wisconsin Road Guide to Haunted Locations*, Terry Fisk and I discovered that back in 1957 a young boy did indeed die while attending the school. However, death took the young boy at the local hospital, not at the school house.

Inside the old school house rests an aged, dust-covered piano which looks as though it hasn't been played in years. This only adds mystery to those who hear piano music coming from the empty building. Occasionally, someone will be inside the building (illegally) at the right moment and notice that the phantom music is accompanied by the unaided moving of the piano's keys.

The oddness of the area also extends to the church positioned directly across the road from the schoolhouse. Legend tells that many years ago, a dedicated priest became distraught over the planned destruction of his beloved church. Having already put his sweat and tears into the construction of the building, the priest was not afraid to add his blood. In order to stop the impending demolition, the priest grabbed a rope, headed to the belfry and ended his own life, providing the passing townsfolk with the gruesome sight of his dangling, lifeless body. Since the unholy day of the priest's death, his body has been spotted hanging from a noose on top of the church. Even though Terry Fisk and I were unable to locate any evidence that supported a suicide at the church, every year dozens of people not only report seeing the hanging spirit of the priest, they also hear the eerie creaking of the phantom noose as it sways back and forth in the wind.

Legend-trippers should also be aware of the phantom headlights that have terrorized scores of visitors who dare venture out to Caryville at night. It is said that long ago, a young woman was coming home from the prom. She had been drinking and drunkenly lost control of her vehicle as it careened into the nearby stream. Unable to free herself from the vehicle, the young woman met her grave in the churning water. Now, unsuspecting travelers crossing paths with Caryville report being chased by bright headlights that race toward them at incredible speeds, only to disappear before the witnesses can make out who or what it is. It seems a bit ironic that these phantom lights are responsible for chasing more people out of Caryville than the local police.

If the abovementioned legends were not enough for you, rest assured more sinister supernatural activity is afoot. Perhaps the scariest and most frightening legend of Caryville is that of a dark, menacing shadow being dubbed "Blackie." One of the most feared of Blackie's antics takes place when curious legend-trippers park their cars near the old school house. While stationary, several

CASE 2 – BLACKIE – THE SHADOW BEING OF CARYVILLE

visitors have reported having their vehicle attacked and shaken by some sort of shadow demon.

*Blackie –
The shadow being of Caryville.*

When Blackie is not busy unnerving parked visitors, he/it tends to show a more playful side by showing up and engaging in what appears to be some sort of twisted game of hide and seek. Often when spotted, Blackie will disappear into the night, only to quickly re-appear in the opposite direction. One eyewitness to Blackie's hijinks was a gentleman who was out exploring Caryville with some friends. While moseying around the outside of the schoolhouse, he spotted a tall, dark shadow resembling the general shape of a man that quickly faded into the night. Once inside the schoolhouse, the group was busy investigating the old piano when the shadow creature appeared in the corner of the building, hunched over as though it was kneeling down. Somehow, the creature had gotten inside the schoolhouse without attracting any notice from the group.

Apart from his apparent playfulness, Blackie also has a penchant for travel, as evidenced by the multiple sightings at the nearby Meridean boat landing and the Sand Hill Cemetery. Each sighting happens in roughly the same manner: a witness catches a glimpse of a shadowy being out of the corner of their eye and, thinking that their eyes are playing tricks on them, they turn to gain a better look at the shadow, only to discover it is no longer visible.

Over the years, I have spent countless nights prowling the area around Caryville in search of the unexplained, and although my personal paranormal experiences there have been limited, I always felt that there was an eeriness residing just out of reach of my investigations. With phantom headlights, hanging priests, spectral music, and, of course, a demon shadow being, Caryville provides legend-trippers with one hell of a cool spot to visit.

CASE 3 – THE SHADOW DEMON OF NEKOOSA

Shadow Demon of Nekoosa

Where To Encounter It:

Greenwood Cemetery
Nekoosa, WI

Directions:

From Nekoosa, take 2nd Street E to the east. Follow it and turn right on 26th Ave. N. (Plank Hill Lane). The cemetery will be on your left.

Creature Lore:

Nearly every culture throughout history has believed in some type of demon or devil-like creature. In the United States, the traditional idea of demons is that of an unholy beast created by, controlled by, and driven by the Devil himself. The physical manifestation of these creatures often vary widely and include everything from a hideous-looking beast to that of a sweet, young girl, possessed by an evil spirit. One can only speculate at the true motives of these creatures, although their goals have never been portrayed in a positive light. Some researchers have put forward the belief that these demons are ultimately looking to steal the souls of unsuspecting humans. If true, I'm not sure a cemetery filled with long-deceased humans would provide the best opportunity to harvest fresh souls, but then again, I am not privy to demon protocol, so maybe it is best if you approach Greenwood Cemetery at your own risk.

History of Lore:

Most people consider cemeteries the exclusive stomping ground for ghosts and spirits, yet every once in a while I will hear of a cemetery encounter that involves something completely outside of the norm. A shadow demon creature using the maintenance shed as it lair certainly qualifies as being outside normalcy. During my research into this case, I was unable to gather any paranormal accounts that pre-date the 1961 encounter. Perhaps sightings of this creature do indeed date back further into history, but if they do, they haven't been discovered. The 1961 story was only known among a few locals until it was told to Rick Hendricks a few years back. Today, the story of the shadow demon can be located on numerous websites and is even scattered among many of the books dealing with paranormal events in WI.

CASE 3 – THE SHADOW DEMON OF NEKOOSA

Investigation Log:

I first became aware of the Nekoosa Shadow Demon when paranormal researcher Richard D. Hendricks shared the case about a hellish, howling demon roaming around the secluded Greenwood Cemetery.

Shed that the shadow demon uses as a lair.

On one of our legend trips, Rick guided us out to the Greenwood Cemetery. Needless to say, I was pretty excited about the opportunity to investigate a demon. I had previously been to more than a few alleged portals to hells. I searched for the Devil child of Illinois, I had chased Hellhounds over several countries, I had even been in the same room that the Devil was once thought to have occupied, yet in all of my strange travels, the chance to check out a demon had somehow alluded me. As we were inspecting the cemetery, Rick began recounting a story from his extensive paranormal casebook. The year was 1961, and three brave teenagers found themselves entwined in October's hypnotic supernatural spell as they decided to drive out to Greenwood Cemetery as the daylight was departing. Just at dusk, the trio arrived at the entrance of the cemetery and quickly parked their car. Suddenly, the heavy main gate swung open as though some unseen force was daring them to enter. At the very same moment, a hellish howl sprang out from the corners of the cemetery. Rising to the challenge, the group entered the sacred ground and began looking around. It didn't take long for the group to spot a six-foot-tall shadowy figure standing near one of the tombstones. The group carefully watched as the unholy creature appeared and disappeared, moving effortlessly among the old gravestones. Moments later, the group spied the creature stomping down on a freshly dug grave as it let out a ghoulish scream of delight. Determined not to be the creature's next victims, the men scurried to their car and darted off to a local bar, where they breathlessly re-told their experiences to a pair of skeptical friends. Figuring that the best way to convince their disbelieving friends was to let them see for themselves, the two-car brigade headed back through the darkness to the cemetery. Not overly eager to set foot back in the cemetery, the men shined their headlights into the seemingly empty graveyard. When nothing out of the ordinary occurred, the group was forced to cross over and walk back through the gates. Back in the corner of the cemetery, the group stumbled upon a rundown, old caretaker's storage shed that appeared to be abandoned. Gazing at the eerie structure, the group noticed the front door had slowly creaked open and standing in the doorway was the shadow demon. It let out a petrifying howl that rattled the group so deep in their bones that they ran off, got into their car and tore out of the area as fast as possible, vowing never to return.

CASE 3 – THE SHADOW DEMON OF NEKOOSA

The shadow demon.

Rick first learned of this case through the son of one of the men who came face to face with the demon. Outside of the abovementioned story, little else is known about the case. Unluckily, or maybe luckily, the shadow demon did not present itself during our investigation. The graveyard was indeed a creepy place, its eeriness only enhanced by the abandoned shed that provided the perfect hiding place for a demon. Over the last couple of years, the cemetery's shadow demon story has spread widely, attracting hordes of legend-trippers who might want to consider the old adage "be careful for what you wish for."

WISCONSIN ROAD GUIDE TO MYSTERIOUS CREATURES

Jenny, the Sea Serpent of Lake Geneva

Where To Encounter It:

Geneva Lake
Lake Geneva, WI

Directions:

Geneva Lake can be accessed directly behind downtown Lake Geneva. The public beach area provides a wonderful viewing area over the lake.

CASE 4 – JENNY, THE SEA SERPENT OF LAKE GENEVA

Creature Lore:

In the depths of Geneva Lake is a giant scale-covered sea serpent that has been spotted for thousands of years. Described by witnesses as a mammoth snake-like creature, the mysterious monster has been lurking beneath the surface and terrifying visitors to the area for quite some time. Locals say that the creature is some type of dinosaur descendant that was passed over by time and evolution. Over the decades, reports of this underwater dweller have continued to baffle both researchers and tourists alike.

History of Lore:

Today Lake Geneva is a bustling resort town overflowing with tourists and seasonal residents. Situated only mere miles from the Illinois border, Lake Geneva flourishes from the steady influx of Chicagoans desperate for a vacation. Yet, long before the area was bombarded by tourists, Native Americans took advantage of the area's fertile farming lands and access to the waters of Geneva Lake. It is estimated that tribes were living in Lake Geneva as far back as 1000 B.C. While no recorded evidence of the natives encountering the mysterious creature inhabiting Geneva Lake has yet been discovered, one piece of possible evidence was destroyed during development. Years ago in Lake Geneva sat two effigy mounds that were believed to have been constructed by unknown native hands. While one of the mounds was shaped in the form of a panther, the other posed an even greater mystery, as it was constructed in the shape of a giant serpent or lizard. Was this effigy mound created to record to sightings of a mysterious serpent the tribe had actually encountered, or was it designed for some other purpose? Unfortunately that question will have to remain unanswered due to the fact that years ago, while the area was experiencing expanded growth and development, the effigy mounds were removed, thus relegating their possible secrets to nothing more than speculation.

The first white pioneers visited the area in 1831. Perhaps the white settlers were warned of the sea monster by the indigenous people, because reports of the unknown sea monster quickly followed. Those who live in the area believe that even though much of the native people's presence has all but disappeared, the belief that a sea serpent inhabits the waters of Geneva Lake continues on. In order to shed some light on the legend we must first examine the lake itself, which is Wisconsin's second largest lake. The expansive lake measures three miles wide, nine miles long, and over 150 feet deep. With such sheer size, the lake offers plenty of room for some unknown creature to reside. Today, the local tourism bureau states that on the bottom of the lake one can find an assortment of odd items including a Volkswagen, a 50's era cabin cruiser, and even the hull of the Lady of the Lake ship. Perhaps with such an established history of mysterious sightings, they can now add the sea serpent to that list.

Does Jenny hide in the waters Geneva Lake?

CASE 4 – JENNY, THE SEA SERPENT OF LAKE GENEVA

Investigation Log:

My first expedition to the area came during the fall, when the area was mostly cleared out of the sunbathing visitors, allowing me to grab a mostly unimpeded view of the lake. The wide lake shore border is composed of both public beach areas and private million dollar lakefront estates. What makes the legend of the lake's large snake-like serpent especially fascinating is the clearness of the waters where it is said to roam. On a good day, the water provides an excellent unimpeded view many feet down. Like most of my investigations, this case began with the need to dig up some additional research on the legend of the serpent. My first stop was the local library, where several of the librarians were puzzled by the request for information on the lake monster. This is nothing new, as many old legends have nearly been forgotten by most. Fortunately, I was directed to a reference librarian who had collected several articles of past sightings. Armed with a good selection of old newspapers on microfilm, and plenty of equipment, the adventure into the Geneva Lake serpent was about to begin.

It is believed that the legend of the Geneva Lake monster dates back to the Native Americans who roamed the land, yet outside of the effigy mounds, no recorded evidence of their sightings has surfaced. Like many other Native American cultures, the stories were passed down through the oral tradition of storytelling. Local tales tell of the Potawatomi believing that in the depths of the lake dwelled a water monster that was formed in the shape of a giant eel or snake. The original inhabitants of the area proceeded with caution whenever they ventured close to the waters. According to legend, their trepidation around the lake was based on prior experiences when canoes were tipped over and sunk by the deadly serpent. If any member of the tribe suddenly went missing, the serpent was the first to receive blame. However, what the natives lacked in officially recording their sightings, the white settlers more than made up for, and so began the modern legend of Geneva Lake's monster that is affectionately known as "Jenny."

While the locals were busy seeing the creature appear all over the lake, the newspapers were equally busy spreading stories of the legend throughout their pages. In 1892, the *Xenia Daily Gazette* briefly touched on the legend, stating that it was an "indescribable monster" that suddenly appeared in Geneva Lake. During the following years it appears as though the creature became very territorial and seemed hell bent on causing trouble for boaters. In his book, *The W-Files,* researcher Jay Rath wrote of several accounts during the 1890s in which unaware boaters would be out enjoying a day on the lake when, out of nowhere, the water would begin to mysteriously boil up around their boat. Within seconds the boaters would find themselves thrown into the waters as some unseen force capsized their boat.

On August 12, 1899, the *Wisconsin State Journal* ran an article that described the lake serpent as being a "thirty-foot monster." With such extraordinary claims coming from all directions, the Geneva Lake monster legend was just getting started.

Even the turn of the century was not enough to slow down the legend, as the early 1900s were especially rife with serpent sightings. In July of 1902, the *Chicago Tribune* covered a magnificent sighting on the banks of the lake. The article tells of Ed Fay, who took two young boys out fishing. The group had spent the day out trolling the lake in hopes of landing a bass or two. As the afternoon wore on the fishermen caught their fill, and the group was about to head back to enjoy their catch when "suddenly there arose out of water within a few rods of the boys the monstrous head of a huge serpent

CASE 4 – JENNY, THE SEA SERPENT OF LAKE GENEVA

with large, fierce-looking eyes and wide open mouth, in which they could plainly see several rows of shard, hooked teeth." Amazingly, the creature raised its head a clear 10 feet out of the water and slowly crept toward the boys. Nearly paralyzed with fear, the trio huddled together as they saw the creature's fish-like scales reflect off the glaring sun. As the beast got closer, the boys were able to see that while the underbelly of the beast was greenish in color, its back was completely black. With the beast now within feet of the boat, the boys' fear nearly consumed them as they waited for the beast to attack. Yet, almost as though it could sense the fear in the air, the serpent let out a thunderous roar, unexpectedly turned course and darted off for the center of the lake. Still dazed from the whole experience, it took the guys several moments before they got the nerve to retreat to the safety of the shore. Once back on the land, the boys immediately told their experience to other witnesses who were gathered around the shore line. According to the group, the creature was all of 100 feet long and was a staggering 3 feet in diameter at its largest spot. As the boys swore they would not return to the lake, other onlookers reported losing sight of the beast near Kaye's Park. Word of the unbelievable serpent story quickly spread, and within hours the banks of the lake were swarming with hundreds of excited onlookers hoping to catch a glimpse of the magnificent beast of the lake.

A drawing of the encounter that appeared in the Chicago Tribune in 1902.

A few months later on September 28, 1902, the serpent made another surprise appearance in broad daylight. Mrs. Buckingham was sitting on the porch of her cabin near Reid's Park, when she noticed a strange serpent coiling and roiling not too far from the shoreline. Mrs. Buckingham could not believe her eyes and stated that the creature had to be at least 65 feet in length, with a perfectly round body that expanded nearly 10 inches in diameter. Whatever the creature was, it was moving through the water with an undulating motion that splashed the water and sent out waves in all directions. The commotion quickly attracted a half-dozen other witnesses who reported that only portions of the creature's body could be seen on the surface of the water. In all her life, Mrs. Buckingham had never seen such a monstrosity and called out to her neighbor, Mrs. Dorliska Reid, to alert her of the beast. Mrs. Reid's two young children, along with another boy, came running to the scene. Upon spotting the creature, the brave young men hurriedly grabbed a row boat and gave chase to the serpent with hopes of obtaining a closer

CASE 4 – JENNY, THE SEA SERPENT OF LAKE GENEVA

look. Perhaps the snake sensed the young men's approach, as it made one last noisy splash before it quickly disappeared into the depths of the lake. Based on several accounts and varying angles, witnesses confidently placed the length of the water monster to be between 25 and 80 feet. On September 29, 1902, the *Janesville Gazette* ran the following story: *Lake Geneva Sea Serpent*. Here the reporter touted the creature as being "sixty-five feet long and from eight to ten inches in diameter." This sighting portrays the serpent as more of a snake-like creature than the traditional sea serpent shape. With multiple sightings occurring every year, the townsfolk dubbed the odd lake inhabitant "Jenny" in honor of their lake.

Eventually the sea serpent craze began to subside. A 1906 *Janesville Daily Gazette* article actively sought out reports of the monster when it asked, "Where are all of the sea serpent and fish stories of the present summer? Both Lake Delavan and Lake Geneva have thus far been free from that awful horror." It seemed like a poignant question, as through the years the number of sighting continued to decrease.

Not all who visited Lake Geneva were firm believers of Jenny's existence. In 1902, the *Lake Geneva Herald* ran an article touting its belief that the serpent was a fake, dreamt up by Chicago journalists in order to sell more newspapers. The article even called into question the sobriety of the "so-called witnesses." More recent skeptics point to the lake's crystal clear waters as evidence disputing the existence of any underwater monster, claiming that any large creature inhabiting the lake would have no place to hide and therefore would have already been caught. However, others believe the bottom-dwelling anomaly rarely surfaces, and when it does, it usually gets spotted by tourists.

Perhaps the most intriguing aspect of the original sightings was the unusual shape of the animal. Instead of having the traditional sea serpent shape complete with humps, Jenny appeared to be more of elongated serpentine-like creature with an unusually lengthy large body. I took great note of this fact as I planned another expedition to Geneva Lake. My second expedition to the lake came in the summer of 2010, when the town was at its peak population. While searching the lake for an open space to watch for the serpent, I encountered various reactions from the visitors when I asked about the lake's paranormal history. Unfortunately, many of the newcomers had never heard of the old serpent legends. Over the years, occasional sightings pop up and are discussed by the old timers, but nothing has yet matched the scope and appeal of the early sightings. After several days of scouring the lake, I finally departed without any substantial evidence of the serpent, yet even so, I continue to hope that somewhere out there Jenny is still scaring unsuspecting tourists.

CASE 5 – PEPIE OF LAKE PEPIN

Pepie-The Serpent of Lake Pepin

Where To Encounter It:

Lake Pepin – Pepin, WI
www.pepie.net

Directions:

Lake Pepin runs along Wisconsin's western border with Minnesota. There are several great viewing areas and public lake access from Bay City, WI all the way down Highway 35 (Great River Road) to Pepin.

Creature Lore:

Something unknown is lurking in Lake Pepin, and for over 140 years this mysterious creature has inhabited the largest lake on the Mississippi River. Just what this bizarre monster is remains unknown, as accounts seem to vary from witness to witness. The Native Americans believed that it was a dangerous killer, the old pioneers believed it was an undiscovered species, and modern vacationers see it as a tourist draw. Each year the long list of eyewitnesses continues to grow, while the answer to what this puzzling creature really is remains as far away as it ever has.

History of Lore:

Tales of the expansive lake hosting some unknown water beastie date back to the Native Americans who first settled near the area. Legend tells of the Natives holding a healthy respect for the many mysteries of the lake. Their respect eventually turned to avoidance after numerous canoes were attacked and punctured by some large water beast. The beautiful waters of Lake Pepin quickly gained the reputation of a place that housed something dark and deadly.

Although oral tales of the creature date back much further, the first recorded sighting of the creature took place on April 24, 1871. According to the April 26 edition of the *Wabasha County Sentinel*, local residents Giles Hyde and C. Page Bonney reported seeing a large unidentified marine monster in the lake. The sensational sighting reported that the creature was between the size of an elephant and rhinoceros, and it moved with great rapidity. The newspaper also stated that on several prior occasions the creature had also been spotted, but no further details were given. The possibilities of the true origin of the creature were endless; the paper even speculated that "the water in the lake is known to be very deep, whales might live in

CASE 5 – PEPIE OF LAKE PEPIN

- but this is not likely to be a whale." Other newspapers picked up and expanded on the case, as the *Titusville Herald* out of Pennsylvania stated that Lake Pepin was "infested with a marine monster." While no definitive explanation of the creature was purposed, two aspects of the monster were widely agreed upon—it was big, and it was fast.

In 1875, the creature made several other spectacular appearances. The *Pierce County Herald* told of a couple of strange sightings that took place in July. The details of the first sighting are lacking, as unfortunately the paper only stated that a monster of some kind was spotted opposite Lake City, Minnesota. The second account is a bit more detailed and tells of Mr. Hewitt and two boys who were out sailing from Lake City to Wacouta in a skiff, when about halfway to their destination, a "dark, strange-looking object rose out of the lake about six feet high at the stern of the boat." The beast remained out of the water long enough for the trio to get a detailed look at it before it disappeared into the depths of the lake. Again, the paper failed to list specific details such as its color, type of body, or other identifying marks, and while most of the town was buzzing with the monster news, not all were believers in Pepie. Several skeptical residents believed that the mysterious sighting was nothing more than a regular lake occupant of natural origin, similar to the four-foot-long, five and a half pound eel that had been captured in the lake just prior to the sighting.

Throughout the early 1900s, the sea serpent legend calmed down a bit and, like most legends, it was nearly forgotten. It wasn't until more recent sightings started occurring that the rich history of the lake brought the creature back into the limelight.

Investigation Log:

Having been on several expeditions in search of the Loch Ness Monster, I was immediately struck by the uncanny similarities that

Lake Pepin shares with the infamous Scotland Loch. Both bodies of water are approximately 23 miles long, both are over a mile wide, and both are surrounded by beautiful bluffs. Although Lake Pepin is not quite as deep as Loch Ness, there is still plenty of room for aquatic mysteries to live. And while many experts believe that Loch Ness does not have a sufficient food source to sustain a population of large sea serpents, Lake Pepin is widely recognized for its plentiful fishing and would have no problem providing for a family of creatures.

Adding even more credibility to the sea serpent legend is the fact that throughout history Lake Pepin's huge body of water has been filled with many other large aquatic animals. On August 10, 1891, the *Eau Claire Weekly Leader* ran the headline, "A Big Fish." The story told of a shovel-nosed sturgeon that had been caught in Lake Pepin. The sturgeon's 16 pound head was described as the largest head ever seen in the area. The fish itself weighed well over 85 pounds. Certainly a fish of this size could have caused quite a disturbance on the lake, leading many to believe that the sturgeon was solely responsible for many of the sea serpent sightings.

Something big moving in the middle of the lake.

CASE 5 – PEPIE OF LAKE PEPIN

The February 2, 1918 edition of the *La Crosse Tribune and Leader Press* featured a story of a mammoth sheephead fish being netted out of Lake Pepin. While a normal sized sheephead in the lake averaged one and a quarter pounds, this whopper weighed over 24 pounds. Even more remarkable than the weight was the sheer size of the fish, which measured over three feet long and had a girth of over one foot. If seen at the right distance, this giant sheephead certainly could have seemed like a large serpent.

The official Pepie website showcases several of the more interesting sightings that have been complied over the years. One such sighting took place on July 9, 2008. At approximately 10am, a motorist was traveling along on Highway 61 and noticed a very large creature moving parallel to the Lake City Beach. The witness pulled over to snap a photo of the creature, which was estimated to be somewhere between 30 and 40 feet long. After snapping the photo, the witness watched the creature slowly disappear back into the water.

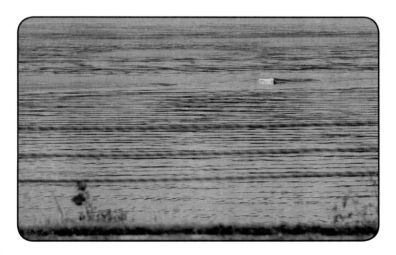

Photo taken in 2008 by motorist who noticed something strange in the water

On one of my expeditions to Lake Pepin, I spoke with a woman who vividly remembered her bizarre sighting of Pepie. On August 21, 2010, the woman and her husband were traveling along Highway 61 on the Minnesota side of the lake when something odd caught her attention. From the passenger window, she gazed out at Lake Pepin and noticed something moving in the water that resembled the long neck and head of a serpent. Not quite believing what she was seeing, the woman jokingly told her husband that she had just seen something that looked like Pepie. Her husband briefly turned his attention from the road to the lake and spotted the same creature. The couple estimated that, whatever the creature was, it had a neck and head that was sticking a good two feet out of the water. It also appeared that the head was attached to a larger body that was mostly submerged under the water. The sighting only lasted a few seconds, and the heavy traffic on 61 forced the couple to keep moving. It all happened so fast that they were not truly sure if they could believe their own eyes. The couple discussed the possibility that what they had seen was a dead log or other floating debris, and like so many others who have witnessed something strange in Lake Pepin, the couple chalked their sighting up as an unsolved mystery.

Postcard of the elusive Pepie.

CASE 5 – PEPIE OF LAKE PEPIN

It is safe to say that the various fish listed above undoubtedly accounted for some of the sightings throughout the years. Yet, it is equally safe to say to state that based on the sheer size and scope of the beast reported by eyewitnesses that something other than a few large fish has been living in the depths of Lake Pepin. Much to their credit, on the other side of the lake, the town of Lake City has embraced the legend of Pepie. In fact, the downtown store of Treats & Treasures is an Official Pepie Watch Station and contains a lot of Pepie merchandise. I spoke with the shop's owner, who informed me that over the years many people have ventured into her store with their personal Pepie sightings. Local business owner Larry Nielson runs the Pepie website and is a wealth of knowledge on the history and sighting of the creature. Nielson and the town are so convinced that Pepie is real that they are offering a $50,000 reward to anyone who can capture proof of its existence.

WISCONSIN ROAD GUIDE TO MYSTERIOUS CREATURES

The Monster in Devil's Lake

Where To Encounter It:

Devil's Lake State Park
S5975 Park Road
Baraboo, WI
(608) 356-8301

Directions:

Devil's Lake is really only accessible from Devil's Lake State Park. To get there from Baraboo, head south on Highway 12 for several miles until you hit Highway 159. Turn left on 159 and follow it to Highway 123. Turn right on 123 and follow it into the park.

CASE 6 – THE MONSTER IN DEVIL'S LAKE

Creature Lore:

In the early days, Wisconsin was overflowing with state-wide reports of terrifying sea beasts. From the oral histories of the Native Americans to the written reports of early settlers, people from all over Wisconsin were spotting these marine monsters in their lakes, rivers, and streams. Resort towns considered these sightings a boom for business, because vacationers flocked to the water for an opportunity to see these bizarre animals. These unusual sightings continued all the way through the 1920s and '30s, at which point they suddenly ceased. Whether people stopped seeing these beasts, or if the newspapers simply quit reporting on them, Wisconsin's sea serpents swiftly disappeared. Slowly, the deadly reputations of these creatures that had been building for decades began to fade into oblivion.

History of Lore:

Since its discovery, Devil's Lake has been surrounded in mystery and legend. Even its name sparks intrigue among historians, who struggle to decipher its true meaning. The Winnebago (now Ho-Chuck) named the lake "Ta-wa-cun-chuk-dah," meaning "Sacred Lake." Other popular translations include: Holy Lake, Mystery Lake, Spirit Lake, Wild Beauty Lake, and Bad Spirit Lake. The name "Devil's Lake" seemed to be one of the more sensational translations accepted by the entrepreneurial business and tourism folks. The major obstacle in the translation lies with the lack of early records from the first settlers of the land. Studies of the area indicate that a band of Natives probably lived near the lake approximately 10,000 to 12,000 years ago. These early tribes were the ones responsible for the effigy mounds that are scattered throughout the park. Eventually the Ho-Chuck Tribe settled in the region. According to the book, *A Lake Where Spirits Live,* one of the earliest recorded sightings of the tribe came in 1846 when the pioneer physician, Dr. Charles Cowles, encountered a native fishing village along the lake.

The early natives told amazing tales of the lake's origin along with numerous other supernatural occurrences. Legend tells that the lake was formed when the giant thunderbirds (Wakhakeera) engaged in a heated battle with the water monsters (Wakunja) who lived in a den in the depths of the lake. The great birds flew high above the land and hurled their thunderbolts down into the waters; the water monster shot up giant rocks and waterspouts from the deeps of the lake. The fight raged on for days. The effects of the battle ravished the land, trees were blown down, rocks were split open, and the land was torn up. Finally, the thunderbirds prevailed and journeyed back to their nest in the north. It was said that no native dared approached the lake for quite some time. Although they lost the battle, not all of the water monsters were killed, and those survivors continue to live in Devil's Lake. A 1964 article in the *Capital Times* stated that for years "it was the custom of the early Indians to make tobacco offerings to the spirits of the lake."

Another legend of the lake tells of a green dragon that lived in the center of the lake. This all-powerful creature was equipped with seven heads and a body that no arrow could pierce. The natives believed that the dragon was the creator of the lake, and he demanded continual offerings which included an annual sacrifice of a fair maiden. The tribe became resentful of the creature's insatiable appetite for tributes and sought out a way to rid themselves of the greedy beast. The beast did have one weakness -- his brain was located behind the left eye of his middle head, making it vulnerable to attack. A young brave named River-Child set off to challenge the

CASE 6 – THE MONSTER IN DEVIL'S LAKE

beast. Along the way he encountered a group of natives who had also experienced the wrath of the dragon. They listened intently to his plan, and when he was done talking they reluctantly agreed to assist him. They waited until dusk, when the water began to swirl and the dragon began to surface. The braves all aimed their arrows at his eye. Sensing their ability to kill him, the dragon swam after River-Child, only to be captured in his net. After an exhausting battle, River-Child was finally able to best the beast with a swift swipe into the beast's eye. The beast may have been killed, but its spirit can be heard screaming for revenge at the onset of every storm.

A 1924 newspaper headline touting the strange history of Devil's Lake

Investigation Log:

With nearly 1.5 million annual visitors, Devil's Lake State Park enjoys the status of being Wisconsin most visited state park. Sadly, the majority of these visitors are unaware of the lake's mysterious past. During my research investigation at Devil's Lake, I was amazed by the beauty of the area. A heavy fog settled down over the lake as though it was trying to obscure its mysteries. The cold, fog, and feel of the place immediately transported me back to my research into a similar creature of Lough Ree, Ireland. But you don't have to travel over to the Emerald Isle to come face to face with a sea monster—you can just head out to Devil's Lake.

During my first expedition to Devil's Lake, I was hoping to find some strange serpent stories from some of the employees. In what has become an all too common situation while researching cases, I learned that no one from the nature center staff was aware of the lake's supernatural reputation. Luckily, with some persistence, I finally was passed along to the Seasonal Naturalist, Diane Pillsbury, who provided me with a wealth of folklore on the lake.

Devil's Lake stands out from most other serpent hotspots because of the sheer number of different beasts thought to dwell in the waters. Unlike most places that claim to have one type of water beastie, if you believe the reports, Devil's Lake is home to a couple of entirely different monsters.

In 1901, a *Milwaukee Journal* article claimed that an alligator was spotted in the lake. Emerson Loomis saw an animal approximately "two feet long, with four legs and a long tail near Devil's Lake. It disappeared in the lake before he could get closer. He is convinced that it is an alligator."

One octopus-type creature sighting is documented in Scott Francis' book, *Monster Spotters*, where Francis tells of an old Sioux legend. One day a group of eager young braves gathered to depart on a hunting expedition. Just as the canoes were launched, the water around them began to swirl, and in an instant the bubbles exploded into a thrashing of tentacles that quickly arose from the chaos. Before the men could even react, several braves found themselves helplessly tangled in the beast's deadly tentacles. As the monster finally submerged, it took the screaming braves with it. All of the commotion had attracted the attention of the rest of the tribe, which quickly rushed down to the shore, only to witness the watery graves that awaited the sinking tribesmen. These deaths led the tribesmen to use extreme caution when approaching the lake, afraid that the beast would wreak havoc on them, too.

CASE 6 – THE MONSTER IN DEVIL'S LAKE

In his book, *Monster Hunt*, Rory Storm writes about a legend in which the Nakota Tribe encountered a plesiosaur-type monster. The lake was reeling from a long drought that had dried up major portions of the water. While out on a morning trek, several tribesman spotted a huge fish-like creature called a "Hokuwa" that had become trapped on the semi-muddy bottom of the drying lake bed. The hideous looking creature was described as having a very large body with an elongated neck that stretched out to its small head. Even the bravest among the tribe would not get within striking distance of the monster. After a bit, the beast was able to flap its body free and descended back into the depths of the lake. This report would seem to indicate that the creature encountered resembled the common sightings of a plesiosaur-type beast that are frequent at Loch Ness or Lake Champlain.

A few years later on July 11, 1892, the *Chicago Tribune* again reported another plesiosaur-type serpent sighting. The article tells that on July 10th, at around 8pm Col. B.C. Deane "a man of unquestionable veracity," L.E. Hoyt, J.B. Cundah, and F.E. Shults, were out fishing:

"The party was fishing at the southwest part of the lake, near the marsh, and having good luck at that spot concluded to anchor their boats and set their lines. They had done this, and were about to partake of refreshments when a peculiar rippling of the water was noticed about 100 feet distant. Up to this time the water had remained perfectly placid, and this strange disturbance attracted their attention. Gazing in that direction they soon saw the head of an immense reptile as it appeared above the water where the disturbance was first noticed. At first the head was barely visible above the water, but gradually it rose until it stood fully six feet out of the water, and to the part of the body that was at the surface of the water two large fin-like paddles were attached. The reptile did not seem to take the least notice of the fishermen, but its large head swayed from side to side, looking in an opposite direction as if in search of something. It was not long before the object of its search appeared. It was nothing less than a second sea serpent of exactly the same description. The second one made its appearance in the same manner as the first. She stood motionless for a few seconds and then the first one made a terrific plunge toward the other and the two serpents were in mortal combat. They lashed the water to such an extent that the waves came near swamping the boats and the party, pale as death, cut them loose and rowed ashore. Today a party of hunters was organized and started in search of the monsters."

The 1892 sighting was covered in many newspapers around the country. The *Xenia Daily Gazette* of Ohio wrote that "two indescribable monsters appeared in Devil's Lake." The reputation of the lake being a place of unnatural events started to spread. One of the first unofficial sea serpent researchers of Devil's Lake was a Chicago man, W.S. Grubb. On July 11, 1897, the *Chicago Tribune* reported that Grubb "spent many of summer here, is daily on the lookout for a large sea serpent which usually makes its appearance the first week of July, but has failed to show up for the season."

The Chicago Tribune published a drawing depicting the epic 1892 serpent battle.

CASE 6 – THE MONSTER IN DEVIL'S LAKE

Devil's Lake seems to have been affected by the same slowing of sea serpent reports that the rest of the state has experienced over the decades. One would think that with well over 1 million annual visitors, someone would encounter the beast of the lake. However, it should be mentioned that many people who encounter something paranormal tend to keep that information to themselves, in fear that no one will believe them. I have also had people share their stories with me that they have kept secret for 10, 20 or 30 years, because they just didn't know who to tell. My own expeditions to Devil's Lake came up empty-handed, but I can only hope that, if the beasts still do dwell in the lake, someone will eventually encounter them.

The mysterious waters of Devil's Lake

Bozho – The Lake Mendota Sea Serpent

Where To Encounter It:

Lake Mendota
Madison, WI

Directions:

Lake Mendota is located near the University of Wisconsin – Madison, forked by Highways 151 and 113. The lake can be easily accessed through numerous locations, including Marshall Park, Warner Park, Tenney Park, and Governor Nelson State Park. The sightings have occurred throughout the entire lake.

CASE 7 – BOZHO – THE LAKE MENDOTA SEA SERPENT

Creature Lore:

Any good sea serpent researcher has to be wary of regular lake items being misidentified as some unknown sea monster. It sometimes happens that those unfamiliar with a lake's behavior may suddenly believe that an everyday occurrence is actually caused by some supernatural force. The most common culprits for these alleged sightings tend to be floating logs, tipped over boats, waves, swimmers, rocks, other fish, and even other animals. On the flipside of this are those skeptical witnesses who originally thought they were viewing these normal lake objects, only to observe the "objects" come to life and rear their huge head and bodies from the water. In the waters of Lake Mendota, it seems there may be more sea serpents than logs.

History of Lore:

The Native Americans were the first people to dread encountering the beast of Lake Mendota, but it was the white settlers who ultimately gave the sea serpent the moniker "Bozho." Folklorist Charles E. Brown believed that the name "Bozho" was an abbreviated version an Indian hero or God called Winnebozho. Oral legends tell of the giant serpent taking a showerbath in the lake, an action that was thought responsible for the whirling waterspouts that formed over the lake.

Investigation Log:

One of the earliest sightings in Lake Mendota occurred during the 1860s. In his book, *The W-Files,* researcher Jay Rath wrote about the strange experience of W.J. Park and his wife while boating near Governor's Island. The couple was out on a leisurely row around the lake when they pulled up next to what they believed was a floating log. When Park lifted his oar up to smack the log, the water erupted and the "log" dove under the water. Park was convinced that that he and his wife had seen a genuine lake monster, but fearing ridicule, the couple kept the encounter to themselves. It wasn't until many other serpent sightings began to circulate that he finally decided to share his bizarre sighting with others.

June in Madison meant that the town would be bustling with tourists looking to escape to the lake for their family vacations. It was also the busiest time of year for Billy Dunn, who was one of Madison's most infamous fishermen. In 1892, the *Chicago Daily Tribune* recapped Dunn's sensational 1883 encounter with the deadly water monster. According to the newspaper, this is how it happened. Dunn and his wife were out fishing near what was called Livesey's Bluff, when he noticed a black object "moving threateningly towards the boat." As the creature approached, Dunn was able to discern the outline of a large snake as it rose up several feet out of the water. "The forked tongue darting fiercely backwards and forwards," as it mashed its way through the disturbed water. The experienced fisherman was not intimidated as he seized his oar and braced for the attack. The serpent, with a "fierce hiss" shot upon the boat and was quickly greeted by Dunn's trusty oar. Instinct took over and the serpent clamped its "long black fangs" down through the wooden oar. As the beast tried to thrash itself from the entanglement, Dunn swiftly grabbed his side holstered hatchet and began smashing "blow after blow" down on the serpent. Bloodied and beaten, the snake released itself from the oar and sank under the water. Dunn stated that he did not trust himself enough to guess at the length of the monster, yet he did say that "it was of a light greenish color and covered with white spots." My favorite part of this fascinating story is that Dunn was said to have kept the oar, which still had a couple of long black fangs imbedded into it, as a trophy of sorts, reminding him of his victorious battle with Lake Mendota's sea monster. Whatever became of that oar is not known.

Dunn's 1883 encounter with the serpent as shown in the Chicago Daily Tribune.

If you were a sea serpent hunter back in 1892, there would have been no better place for you to conduct your research than Madison's Lake Mendota. On July 25, the *Oshkosh Daily Northwestern* briefly mentioned, "Not long ago a sea serpent was seen in Lake Mendota." It must have been a very busy news day because the article left out all of the pertinent details of the sighting. On August 30, the *Marshfield Times* reported, "Another sea serpent had been seen in Lake Mendota." Once again, the newspaper failed to give specific details of the encounter. Luckily, just over a week later, another more descriptive encounter took place. It was October 6 when local monster hunter John Schott began an organized hunt for what the *Janesville Gazette* called "the slimy denizen of the deep." Schott, who had already encountered the creature on three different occasions, described the creature, stating, "It has a large head, flat on top and square like a box." He claimed that the creature's head stood a good three feet out of the water and was connected to a large

25-foot body, which was partially submerged. Three weeks later, another group of men would corroborate Schott's size estimates. The day was October 28, and the chilly winds of the season had begun to set in when a number of young men braved the harsh fall conditions and set out sailing. Midway through the route, the dozen sailors caught a good view of a huge serpent moving through the water. The *Eau Claire News* wrote, "All of them declare that it was very large. Some say it was fully 35 feet long, others say 30 and the lowest estimate is 25 feet. Not being on a hunt for the serpent they had no firearms and were glad to escape from the monster."

An 1892 newspaper headline from the Racine Daily Journal.

In August of 1899, a group of women were enjoying a relaxing camping expedition along the beautiful banks of the lake. The camping party consisted of Mrs. E. Grove, Mrs. J.J. Pecher, and several additional unnamed women. To help alleviate the effects of the summer heat, the party jumped in their boat and headed out on the cool, refreshing lake. Suddenly, the women noticed something bobbing up out of the water. According to the *Racine Daily Journal,* the women "saw a long, snake-like monster with a head ten inches across, and a tail which had horns." The group was not willing to risk their lives on the hopes of the good intentions of the beast, so they frantically paddled for the safety of the shore. The commotion of their paddling

CASE 7 – BOZHO – THE LAKE MENDOTA SEA SERPENT

evidently scared the creature, which abruptly plunged back into the depths of the lake, creating "a great deal of foam," along with it. Following up on the women's story, the *Wisconsin State Journal* skeptically reported that the six-foot long monster was equipped with two three-inch horns protruding from its tail. The women were not alone in their sighting. That same month another witness saw the monster. The story was summarized in Jay Rath's book, *The W-Files*, and tells of Barney Reynolds, who caught sight of a similar creature near the landing for the Bernard Boat Yard. It is unknown whether both sightings were of the same creature.

In 1942, Charles E. Brown of the Wisconsin Folklore Society put out a booklet titled *Sea Serpents*, detailing Wisconsin's sea serpent past. In the booklet, he devotes the first entry to the many sightings of Bozho. Brown did an amazing job at capturing some essential WI sightings. One of the later sightings occurred in 1917, when a University of Wisconsin student was enjoying the beach area of Picnic Point on the north shore when he stumbled upon what looked like a fish scale. Curious, the student brought the tough scale to his professor who determined that the scale came from the body of a sea serpent. This sensational scale story opened the door for others to report their own odd sightings in the lake. Brown wrote that later in the year a fisherman was trying his luck at a perch off the end of Picnic Point. At a distance of 100 feet out, he spotted a "large snake-like head, with large jaws and blazing eyes emerge from the deep water." The sight was so overwhelming that the man could do nothing but stare at the creature, his own body unwilling to react. Eventually, the man pulled himself together and fled from the shoreline, leaving both his pole and basket behind. Hoping to find an explanation to his sighting, the man shared the account with several of his friends, "but no one believed his story."

Brown's odd collection of Lake Mendota stories ranged from the previous scary encounter to this more humorous tale of a young lady who discovered that the creature was a little too friendly for her liking. Not too long after the abovementioned story, a couple of university students were basking in the sun at the end of a frat house pier. The young man and his female companion were laying face down, letting the sun soak in through their backs. After a few moments, the girl felt something tickling the sole of her foot. Convinced that her friend was the culprit, the woman glanced over at him only to find his eyes were closed in relaxation. The woman brushed off the incident and began to relax. However, a few moments later the tickling resumed, and this time the woman spun over quickly and saw "the head and neck of a huge snake, or dragon" extended above the water. The woman reported that it "had a friendly, humorous look in its big eyes." The creature had been using its long tongue to caress the feet of the sun-bathing girl. She quickly grabbed her friend, and they scurried back to the safety of the frat house.

Brown also included several less detailed stories of the serpent overturning canoes, chasing sailboats, and frightening bathers. He wrote that for the most part this serpent was "a rather good-natured animal," whose pranks were basically harmless. Brown also made the distinction between these mischievous serpent sightings and the more sinister "old Indian water spirits, long-tailed, horned, cat-like animals believed to have a den in the deep water of Governor's Island on the north shore of the lake."

CASE 7 – BOZHO – THE LAKE MENDOTA SEA SERPENT

The peaceful waters of Lake Mendota.

With so many credible sightings taking place, one could easily wonder why no hard evidence of the creature has been found. Lake Mendota has been called the most studied lake in America and even contains a remote sensor buoy in its waters used by the University of Wisconsin, and during the summer, the lake is highly used by an assortment of people. You would think that the commotion of the boaters, swimmers, and those fishing would stir up these large creatures, yet year after year goes by without so much as a hint of a credible sighting. Skeptics claim that the reported sea serpents were nothing more than a pickerel or garfish with a head full of fishing lures scaring all the naïve tourists. Regardless of the explanation, the mystery of Lake Mendota continues on. Maybe someday someone will find Billy Dunn's fang-filled oar, and the mystery can be solved once and for all. Until that day comes, grab your bait and head over to Lake Mendota.

WISCONSIN ROAD GUIDE TO MYSTERIOUS CREATURES

The Lake Monona Sea Serpent

Where To Encounter It:

Lake Monona
Madison, WI

Directions:

Lake Monona is not too far from the Capitol Building, just southeast of Lake Mendota as you cross over Highway 151. The lake can be accessed in numerous spots, including Olin and Olbrich Parks, along with many trails.

CASE 8 – THE LAKE MONONA SEA SERPENT

Creature Lore:

Not everyone was caught up in the sea serpent fever of the late 1800s and early 1900s. Skeptics claimed that these so-called monsters were nothing more than regular fish that were being misidentified. Skeptics rolled out a number of possible fish that, on any given day, could have been mistaken for a giant marine monster. The most commonly-blamed fish were the Sturgeon, Oarfish, Muskie, and Northern Pike. Some even thought large turtles were at the heart of serpent sightings. However, what seems to expose this theory was the absolute certainty with which the witnesses believed that whatever they had seen was not merely some normal animal. Adamant in their convictions, the witnesses believed that something unknown really did/does lurk in Lake Monona.

History of Lore:

In the 1860's, the city of Madison aspired to expand from the Capitol City into a major regional hub of trade, commerce, and tourism. Lakeside hotels and resorts started springing up to entice weary travelers and vacationing families. The ongoing development around Lake Monona spurred some of the first recorded sea serpent reports as the influx of new visitors utilized all portions of the lake. Each summer, as the tourist season grew, so did the reported sea serpent sightings. A credible sighting of a lake monster generated a lot of positive publicity, which in turn drew more tourists, who of course saw more serpents. The whole cycle fed on itself for many years until the reports started to dwindle, and the sea serpent seemed lost to history.

Investigation Log:

As evidenced by the rash of serpent sightings in nearby Lake Mendota, 1892 was a good year for Madison monster hunters, and Lake Monona would not disappoint. "Madison's Lake Snake is Twenty Feet Long," read the June 11, 1892 *Janesville Gazette* article. Norman Morgan was out fishing when he spotted what appeared to be a soaked log lying in the water. "As he sat there looking at the thing he saw one end of it rising out of the water a bit." Bravely, Morgan stood up in his boat and put one of his feet over the side and let it rest on the "log." Just as soon as his foot touched down, Morgan saw that the log was actually a serpent as "large as a telephone pole," with a mouth as large as a barrel. The creature dashed backwards, showing a mouth so big that Morgan claimed, "You could have run a wheel barrel into it." The beast was widely splashing around as though it was trying to get into the boat. In fact, the beast's tail had whipped up so much water that Morgan "was afraid the boat would go down." At a time when most people would have high-tailed it out of there, Morgan grabbed a big hunting knife and went after the creature, stabbing the serpent an estimated forty times. Unfortunately, this is where the article inexplicably ends, leaving us to ponder what happened next and the ultimate fate of the serpent.

There was also a rash of similar sightings that got much less publicity.

On July 21, Darwin Boehmer and a friend spotted the creature while out on a boat ride. In his book, *The W-Files*, Jay Rath, writes that Boehmer saw the creature moving along the south shore at a good pace. The creature got within 75 feet—so close, in fact, that the men could see that the beast was "undulating in an up-and-down motion. Its head, they said, resembled that of a dogfish." Several

CASE 8 – THE LAKE MONONA SEA SERPENT

There have been several close encounters with the Lake Monona serpent.

others had witnessed the beast from the shore and estimated that it was approximately 10 -15 feet long. A few days later, on July 25, the *Oshkosh Daily Northwestern* wrote that the creature was "heading for the campgrounds of the Monona Lake assembly when seen." Jay Rath wrote of another bizarre 1892 sighting. It was October 7 when an anonymous man rented a boat from John Schott (who also had seen the beast). The man was rowing about and having a good time, when all of a sudden a 20-foot-long monster passed underneath his boat. The man panicked because he believed the creature was attempting to capsize the boat and quickly rowed back to the safety of the shore. He vowed never to return to the lake without some handy weapons.

Over the next few years other similar sightings took place, but they received a lot less publicity. On August 24, 1894, the *Janesville Daily Gazette* simply wrote, "Madison's sea serpent has been resurrected."

On June 11, 1897, Lake Monona was again abuzz with news of a spectacular encounter with a sea serpent. The whole episode began when a crowd of onlookers noticed a 20-foot beast traveling along the surface of the lake. The next day the *Wisconsin State Journal* ran the article "What-Is-It-In The Lake?" and wrote that the beast "traveled east on the surface of the lake until Eugene Heath, agent of the Gaar-Scott company, fired two shots into it, when it turned and came back." What happened next is unsure because "either the snake or the spectators appeared to have disappeared." The Journal interviewed Mr. Schott, an eye witness, who claimed that "its appearance is not that of a serpent…and that its shape was like the bottom of boat, but it was about twice as long." The article goes on to state that Mr. Schott's two sons also caught a glimpse of the beast and "were so firmly convinced that it was a dangerous animal that when two ladies desired to be rowed over to Lakeside neither of the Schotts, who had spent a large part of their lives on the lake, would venture out." Even more amazingly, the paper claimed that the serpent was "probably the same animal which is credited with having swallowed a dog which was swimming in the lake a few days ago." All of the witnesses insisted that what they saw was real and not a joke or some figment of their imagination. The *Wisconsin State Journal* wrote, "In these years a curious monster, perhaps the same sea serpent, was also observed off the Tonywatha and Winnequah resort shore, on the east side of the lake, by different persons."

The expansive Lake Monona.

CASE 8 – THE LAKE MONONA SEA SERPENT

So, what happened to all of Madison's sea serpents? One theory claims that they may have all died out, pointing to a story that tells of construction workers dredging off of the Olbrich Park shore when a heavy sand pump pipe became clogged. Workers went to inspect the situation and found several huge vertebrae trapped in the machine. It was believed that these vertebrae were the remains of a deceased sea serpent. Others believe that water demons still reside in the lake and make themselves known to any legend-tripper willing to put in the necessary time.

WISCONSIN ROAD GUIDE TO MYSTERIOUS CREATURES

Lake Ripley's Serpent

Where To Encounter It:
Lake Ripley
Cambridge, WI

Directions:
Lake Ripley is located in Cambridge, WI. Much of the lake is surrounded with private resorts, family cabins and summer homes. However, there are several public access points including the wonderful Ripley Park. From Cambridge, head east on Highway 18, turn right on park road and follow it down until you see Ripley Park on your left.

For those of you looking to experience the serpent in style, you also have the option of staying at the Lake Ripley Lodge B&B, which is located right on the lake.

CASE 9 – LAKE RIPLEY'S SERPENT

Creature Lore:

The creature inhabiting Lake Ripley is a bit difficult to classify due to the varying accounts of its shape and size. On one hand, there are plenty of witnesses who have spotted a long snake or worm-like creature in the lake. On the other hand are the witnesses who have caught glimpses of something that resembled more of the traditional serpent-like shape (think Loch Ness Monster). Maybe people were seeing several different creatures. It may seem far-fetched, but perhaps if/when the Red Cedar Lake monster moved to Lake Ripley, there was already something else there.

History of Lore:

By nearly all accounts, the serpent activity on Lake Ripley began in the summer of 1891. It was thought to be caused by the diminishing water depths of nearby Red Cedar Lake. Locals theorized that the creature that had been spotted so often in Red Cedar Lake had traveled to the deeper Lake Ripley through an underground water channel that was thought to connect the two lakes.

Confusing the timeline a bit is a 1945 article from the *Wisconsin State Journal* that contends that the first sighting of the Lake Ripley monster occurred not in 1891, but in 1861. It tells of two witnesses, Newton Hart and Norman Porter, who were out fishing near the lake's island. The men noticed a "giant animal or fish" come out of the waves. "The serpent had a head the size of a horse's," and was shaped like that of a rattlesnake. The two men stated that the beast went wild—lashing its tail while water sprayed from it nostrils. The creature was estimated to be at least four rods (66 feet) long. However, it is my opinion that the 1945 article simply got the date 1861 confused with 1891. I based this opinion on several pieces of evidence. First, I was unable to find any other accounts of a serpent in Lake Ripley or Red Cedar Lake that pre-dates the 1880s. I also discovered that in 1946, Norman Porter celebrated his Golden Anniversary (50 years) with his wife. If we go by the 1861 date, even if Porter was 15 years old when he witnessed the creature (even though the article did not list him as young man or youngster) it would mean that he was 100 at the time of his anniversary. It would also mean he didn't marry until he was 50 years old—all of which doesn't seem to fit the time period. It is much more plausible that the 1945 article simply got the dates mixed up.

Investigation Log:

In the September of 1891, the *Janesville Gazette* wrote that because of the lowering water levels in nearby Red Cedar Lake, "grave fears are entertained that the serpent is about to change its habitation to Lake Ripley." Indeed, many residents along the shore were positive that they had caught a glimpse of "his snakeship." Within a few short years, word of the serpent had spread far and wide. An 1895 blurb in the *Waukesha Freeman* touted a new summer resort that was opening "at Lake Ripley, of sea serpent notoriety."

Plenty of food options for a creature inhabiting Lake Ripley.

CASE 9 – LAKE RIPLEY'S SERPENT

Although no actual human deaths had been attributed to the beast, it was responsible for quite a number of close calls. In 1895, three women were enjoying a quiet September walk along the banks of the lake near dusk. According to the *Chicago Daily Tribune*, "A terrible commotion was seen in the water." Whatever was causing the commotion, it was a bit too close to shore for the ladies' comfort. Even though the creature had never attacked a human, it was now well within striking range and the women were on edge. The group cautiously watched as the commotion got larger and larger until the "women were frightened almost into spasms."

Like so many communities of the 1800s, the townsfolk depended on the frozen lake to provide the town's year-round ice supply. Every winter ice harvesters gathered on the icy lake to begin cutting. The *Chicago Daily Tribune* wrote of an interesting winter encounter that got under the nerves of even the most hardened ice harvester. In 1895, the men were out near the center of the lake inspecting the thickness and quality of the ice, when they "noticed a peculiar wavy black crease, like a mud stain, beneath the surface of the clear ice." Curious, the men followed the brown line for nearly 100 feet. Then "all at once the black seam began to writhe…and although the ice was a foot thick, it began to crack" and sounded like an ice-gorge breaking in a rapid river. Within seconds, the black line disappeared as quickly as it had appeared. The men were so frightened by this mysterious black line that the paper wrote, "Needless to add, the ice-harvesting was done near the shore for the rest of the season." Even near the safety of the shore, the men were a bit tense as they continued to feel strange motions in the water throughout the winter.

The summer of 1896 did not bring any relief to the sightings… in fact, it was a bumper year for the serpent. Luckily for us, the *Chicago Daily Tribune* documented many of the events. To provide some recreation for their guests, several resorts placed floating platforms out in the water. These diving floats were anchored in fifteen feet of water and soon became known as the "monster's playthings." During one July evening just as the sun was setting, one of the floats in front of a hotel suddenly began to rise up into the air. The water around the float was thrashing as many spectators along the shore stated they saw "something like an elephant rise up with the float on its head like a bonnet." Amazingly, witnesses claimed the float was lifted a clean twenty feet out of the water before it "suddenly dropped with a splash which broke a strong chain used for mooring." Later in the same week, the area was expecting a strong storm to touch down. One evening before the storm came in, "a strange rushing noise was heard upon the water." The rushing sound was accompanied by a loud hissing noise like "a cyclone." At that very moment, "something passed over the surface," and witnesses swore it was the giant serpent.

At least one of the local farmers refused to buy into the serpent story. According to the *Chicago Daily Tribune*, "Sheep are being snatched from folds at night on neighboring hillsides." One particular farmer who had lost several of his sheep blamed the killings on dogs. Apparently the farmer would carry a gun with him everywhere, threatening to shoot all the

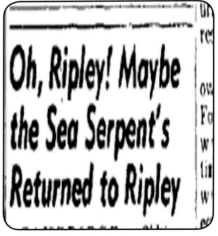

Newspaper headlines like this help fuel the sea serpent frenzy of the early 1900s.

CASE 9 – LAKE RIPLEY'S SERPENT

dogs he could find, even though no dogs were ever seen attacking the livestock. Of course, the paper also mentioned how impossible it would be for a dog to be able to swallow a sheep whole.

After so many sightings of the beast, excursion parties were formed to hunt the serpent, and tourists flocked to the shores in hopes of catching sight of the lake monster.

In 1896, the *Osseo-Eleva Journal* ran an article claiming the Lake Ripley sea serpent was nothing more than a hoax brought upon by a local farmer who believed that stories of a serpent would drive away tourists. Apparently, the farmer was fed up with tourists stomping through his meadows and fields in order to get close to the lake. It is alleged that he made up the story of the beast taking away his livestock to ward off potential visitors. Unfortunately, the plan backfired. Droves of tourists clamored for the chance to vacation on lake with a genuine sea serpent, much "to the poor German's disgust." Articles like these were very common and often popped up after years of sightings. My main concern with this article is the fact that during this time period, sea serpent sightings caused quite a stir and garnered a ton of publicity, which almost always resulted in a marked increase in tourists. It seems highly unlikely that any farmer would believe that a serpent story would actually keep visitors away. I am much more willing to entertain the notion that these stories were created in order to increase tourism, not to discourage it. I know that several researchers and authors have written about how panicked the people of Lake Ripley were and how that chaos resulted in the widespread closing of cabins and resorts along the lake. Yet, according to all of the newspaper accounts of the day, the exact opposite was true, as record crowds who were caught up in the serpent frenzy descended upon the lake.

Unlike many of the other lakes in Wisconsin, Lake Ripley's sightings continued well into the 1940s. On July 19, 1945, the

Janesville Gazette wrote about the resurgence of serpent sightings in the lake. The paper told that many unusual happenings and sounds were being reported by the residents living along the lake. Among these strange happenings was that "a large number of carp had been found in the weeds on the south shore of the lake with huge gashes in their sides." Old-timers also complained that the number of fish in the lake had significantly decreased, the blame being placed on the hungry serpent.

CASE 10 – RED CEDAR LAKE MONSTER

Red Cedar Lake Monster

Where To Encounter It:

Red Cedar Lake
Oakland, WI

Directions:

There are two Red Cedar Lakes in Wisconsin. This one is located in the southern part of the state, between the cities of Oakland and Rockdale. It is part of the Red Cedar Lake State Natural Area and just south of Lake Ripley.

The lake is hard to access by car. From Cambridge, take Highway 12 to the east for twelve miles and then turn right on Brosig Lane (a small access road). The lake is best accessed by a canoe or kayak, or for the very brave, swimming.

Creature Lore:

In my nearly 20 years of researching the paranormal, I have heard a lot of sea serpents stories. I have dug up hundreds of newspaper reports from all over the world, and after a while a lot of these stories start to blend together in their similarities. What I love about the Red Cedar Lake stories is that the creature is not so much a sea serpent as it is a killing machine that devours unwary prey.

History of Lore:

Looking at Red Cedar Lake today, it is hard to imagine that it was once home to some of the most exciting sea serpent encounters in Wisconsin. The main problem with the idea is the shallowness of the lake. According to the Wisconsin DNR, the lake's maximum depth is around 6 feet, while over ninety percent of the lake is less than 3 feet deep. This doesn't leave a lot of room for an eighty- foot monster to maneuver. Yet, back in the 1800s the lake was described as a much deeper body of water, which years of low rainfall and runoff all but drained. Little of the land surrounding the lake has changed, as it is still mostly comprised of farmland, making the lake hard to reach by car. In 1984, the lake was designated a State Natural Area and is currently owned by the Wisconsin DNR.

CASE 10 – RED CEDAR LAKE MONSTER

The swampy shallow shores of Red Cedar Lake.

Investigation Log:

Out of all the serpent stories featured in this book, the Red Cedar Lake encounters rank as some of my favorites. Throughout the book, you will read a lot of stories of witnesses who engaged in bloody battles with lake monsters—everything from a man smashing a serpent with his oar, a fisherman stabbing a serpent, and even a witness firing his gun at a serpent. This case, however, is the only one where the serpent takes revenge on anything and everything that it can.

On August 15, 1890, the *Oshkosh Daily Northwestern* described a deadly encounter with the beast. A Red Cedar Lake farmer was horrified as he watched a "reptile forty feet long carry off one of his hogs." The paper speculated that the deadly lake monster was the same creature that had been spotted in 1880, when it was only ten feet in length.

It didn't take long for the creature to receive a deadly reputation as a ferocious killer. This well-earned reputation was only enhanced by the media reports of the day. One of my favorite articles came on September 5, 1891, when the *Janesville Gazette* ran this entertaining piece:

> The cedar lake sea serpent is again making trouble. When first seen, about ten years ago, the serpent was variously estimated at from thirty to forty feet in length, but now it cannot be less than eighty feet long. This year it has been particularly destructive of young pigs and lambs which might be feeding near the banks of the lake, sometimes running nearly half the length of its body on the land to seize its prey. It has never been seen but once with its body entirely upon land, and some doubts are expressed as to the truthfulness of this report, as the man who claims to have been an eyewitness of this occurrence is not noted for his truth and voracity. It is generally seen just at the close of the day or very early in the morning; and when seen with head raised ten feet from the surface of the water, its mouth wide open, and rushing towards the shore, its appearance is apt to carry consternation to the stoutest nerves. When it comes to curiosities, this section of Wisconsin is bound not to be undone by any other part of the state.

In his booklet, *Sea Serpents*, Folklorist Charles E. Brown wrote of an interesting 1891 encounter. He tells of a fisherman who had just returned home and was tying up his boat. He looked out into the lake and saw a large form undulating through the water. It appeared to be a large snake or fish with its head submerged under the water. The astonished man watched as the creature swam out of sight. Excited, the fisherman told several of his friends and neighbors,

CASE 10 – RED CEDAR LAKE MONSTER

only to discover that others had seen the bizarre marine monster as well. One neighbor described the beast as having a large head with several saw tooth-looking protuberances running down the spine of its back.

The story of the Red Cedar Monster changed in 1891, when locals believed that there existed an underground water passage linking Red Cedar Lake with Lake Ripley to the north. Low rainfall had made Red Cedar Lake extremely shallow. When sightings began to increase in the deeper Lake Ripley, several newspapers picked up on the rumor that the creature had run out of prey at Red Cedar Lake and traveled up to Lake Ripley. The *Janesville Gazette* wrote, "Residents of the banks of the latter lake are positive that they have caught glimpse of his snakeship."

The Red Cedar Lake serpent was perhaps the deadliest of all WI serpents.

If the monster did travel to Lake Ripley, it wasn't gone long, because on June 16, 1892 the *Pocahontas County Sun* ran the article "A Serpentine Monster," telling of several Germans who were out boating on Red Cedar when they spotted a floating log sticking several feet out of the water. The group watched as a large mud turtle climbed upon the log to sun itself, and it turned out that the perceived log was actually a large lake monster. Instead of enjoying some rays, the turtle disappeared into the creature's "capacious mouth." The lake monster must have had a ravenous appetite that wasn't limited to turtles. At the same time the Germans spotted the creature, *The New North* claimed that local farmer, Will Ward, had several of his valuable sheep fall victim to the monster, writing, "Their mangled forms were found in the mud, partly devoured."

However, it should be noted that not everybody was a true believer in the serpent. On August 24, 1894, the *Marshfield Times* poked a bit of fun at the serpent. The area was in the midst of a heat wave that had turned the water of the lake into a "mass of jelly." The paper joked that the jelly must have been caused by the melting of the lake's sea serpent from the extreme heat.

Limited access to Red Cedar Lake provides the perfect hiding spot for a large serpent.

CASE 10 – RED CEDAR LAKE MONSTER

As previously mentioned, the lake is very hard to access without a boat of some kind. As I circled the lake in my car, I did find several high spots on the road that made for a good serpent watching post, but to really see the lake you need to use an access road and get in closer. The lake itself is a pretty good size (370 acres) and is surrounded by wetlands and marshy water that also inhibits easy access. The access road (Brosig Lane) does a good job at getting you to the lake. As I was exploring the lake by myself, my mind started to explore the idea that because the lake was so shallow, a person could almost walk right across the entire thing without having to swim at all. I scoured the area in search of the deadly monster, but once again I came up empty-handed. Regretfully, I did not end up walking across the lake…which is probably why I am still alive today.

Phantom Chickens of Chicken Alley

Where To Encounter It:

Chicken Alley
Seymour, WI

Directions:

From the city of Seymour, go west on City Rd G and turn right on French Road; after approximately 5 miles the road turns left and becomes Chicken Alley.

CASE 11 – PHANTOM CHICKENS OF CHICKEN ALLEY

Creature Lore:

Chicken Alley is a short, lonely stretch of rural road hidden from the prying eyes of most Interstate travelers. Those who make the effort to find this nearly forgotten location are treated to some of the strangest legends Wisconsin can dish up, which makes Chicken Alley a must hit paranormal destination. Throughout my travels around the world I have investigated countless cases involving phantom animals—everything from spectral cats, dogs, birds, and even vanishing kangaroos—yet, when it comes to absolute strangeness and wackiness, Chicken Alley remains at the top of my list.

History of Lore:

No one is quite sure how long the legends surrounding Chicken Alley have been circulating. Often times, legends of this type are only known to a handful of local long-time residents lucky enough to be privy to the guarded information. I first became acquainted with the legends in 1998, when I started receiving reports from witnesses looking for answers to explain their odd encounters at Chicken Alley. It is certainly possible that these bizarre stories date back many, many years, but so far no early tales have yet surfaced.

Investigation Log:

The utter strangeness of Chicken Alley begins as soon as curious sight seekers arrive at the mysterious Chicken Alley street sign. I state that the sign is "mysterious," because the most commonly reported anomaly of the area is the story of people who witness the street sign disappearing right before their eyes. Others firmly believe that on certain nights when the stars are perfectly aligned, both the street sign and street pole will be missing from sight, as though they never existed at all. Still even more bizarre is the claim that if you are lucky enough to catch a glimpse of this vanishing sign, it will be impossible for you to capture its image on a camera, no matter how many times you try, or how many different cameras you use.

Curious sight seekers who visit the quiet area quickly learn that they are not alone on their pursuit of weirdness. Numerous visitors have reported seeing the faint light of an approaching snowmobile coming toward them. As the machine speeds closer, witnesses report that they can actually hear the revving sounds of the engine, and they can make out the outline of the snowmobile as the approaching vehicle's headlight becomes bright. However, just as the snowmobile gets within the range of identifying its operator, it simply vanishes into thin air. To make matters even more complicated, I have received many sightings of the phantom snowmobiles in the heart of the summer. Many who have seen the light claim that it possesses a more sinister motive, and some believe that the light was under the control of some type of intelligence. The most common report of this type that I get goes something like this: A group of friends decide to press their luck and visit Chicken Alley in order to experience all of the alleged happenings of the area. After taking hundreds of photos and convincing one other to take the dare, the group members pile back into their car and begin to set off for the safety of home, relieved that they had survived the journey, when out of nowhere a strange light suddenly races up from behind them. By all accounts the light seems to be chasing their vehicle out of the area. As the terrified group punches the accelerator, the light easily keeps up with the pace. Just when the fear and panic of those in the car becomes palpable, the light vanishes as quickly as it appeared.

CASE 11 – PHANTOM CHICKENS OF CHICKEN ALLEY

The crossroads of Chicken Alley where the dare needs to be completed.

For years, adventurous legend trippers who ventured out to Chicken Alley tested their bravery by pitting themselves against the Chicken Alley Dare. Many paranormal places around the world have these "dares" associated with them. These dares usually consist of some sort of action that needs to be done by the legend tripper in order for the legend to come true. Whether it is visiting a spot at exactly midnight, or having to say the name of the alleged ghost three times, there is some type of established ritual that needs to be completed, and the Chicken Alley Dare is no different. The Chicken Alley Dare is this: if you are foolish enough to stand in the middle of the crossroads between Chicken Alley and Shady Road, the silence of the remote area will be shattered by the angry voice of an unseen man yelling at you to "Get Out Of The Road!" Legend dictates that if you do not heed his advice and vacate the area, you will be cursed with bad luck until the day you die. Those of you who are familiar with folklore will recognize the significance of having to attempt the dare at a crossroads. Throughout history the crossroad has represented a believed portal between our world and the fiery underworld of Hell. Legend states that if you are seeking to sell your soul to the Devil, the unholy deed would have to be conducted at a crossroads, so it seems only fitting that the angry phantom voice of Chicken Alley would haunt the crossroad. Luckily, or maybe unluckily for me, the dozen or so times I waited at the crossroads, no voice yelled at me, and I was fortunately spared from the curse of bad luck.

So as of now, we have the legend of a disappearing/sometimes non-existent street sign, a phantom snowmobile/light that chases away visitors, and an angry disembodied spirit looking to curse you with bad luck. Even with the plethora of bizarre phenomena occurring at Chicken Alley, believe it or not, the story is about to get even weirder with the addition of… phantom chickens. Many unsuspecting travelers cruise down the road when, out of nowhere, a group of chickens dart out in front of their speeding vehicle. Witnesses are shocked to notice that the crossing feathered fowl appear nearly transparent

Keep an eye out for the phantom chickens that haunt Chicken Alley.

CASE 11 – PHANTOM CHICKENS OF CHICKEN ALLEY

and sometimes have a faint glow emanating from them. Inevitably, people get out of the car to assess the damage to their vehicle, or to search for the roadkill, only to discover that no deceased fowl exist. Some are so convinced that they have run over a real chicken that they have even gone so far as to knock on the doors of the few nearby homes inquiring if anyone is raising chickens. Of course when they discover that no chickens are being raised in the area, they depart the area convinced that they had a mysterious encounter with the phantom chickens of Chicken Alley.

WISCONSIN ROAD GUIDE TO MYSTERIOUS CREATURES

Aliens Bring Pancakes

Where To Encounter It:

Highway 70 and Highway 17
Eagle River, WI

Directions:

Joe Simonton lived approximately 4 miles west of Eagle River on Highway 70.

Other sightings took place along Highway 17.

CASE 12- ALIENS BRING PANCAKES

Creature Lore:

The most commonly reported extraterrestrial biological entities (aliens) are that of the "greys." Their bodies are thin and slight, the skin is gray in color and they range from 3-4 feet in height. The most distinguishing feature of these beings is their eyes, which are large, dark, almond shapes which occupy a good portion of the oversized heads. Thanks to Hollywood and the media, this type of alien is the most recognizable to the general public, yet many other alien beings are often sighted. The "Nordic" creatures are tall human-looking beings with blonde hair, blue eyes and perfect bodies. Abductees state that they resemble Scandinavian people. Lesser friendly beings are also reported, and among them is what is known as the "Giant Praying Mantis" type. These creatures resemble the praying mantis found here on earth, just in a much bigger body. Ranging from 5-7 feet tall, with solid black or dark brown bodies, these beings tend to be much less caring and more aggressive toward the abductees than other aliens. Even more frightening in appearance are the "reptilians," which are reported to be 6-8-foot tall snake-like creatures that are covered in reptilian-like scales. Noted abduction researcher John Carpenter likens these beings to a bunch of drunken frat boys out for a night on the town.

In addition to the regularly reported aliens, there are hundreds of bizarre alien-type creatures who have been seen by—and interacted with—humans. These beings are much more difficult to categorize because descriptions of them vary tremendously. While some similarities between these beings do in fact exist, their major differences in size, shape, color, temperament, and perceived motives run the entire spectrum. Researchers are left with reports of the commonly-reported and established creatures, and the other too bizarre and too numerous unlabeled creatures. I feel that it is safe to say that Joe Simonton's encounter with pancake wielding space beings certainly fits into the latter category.

History of Lore:

"Is Wisconsin stranger than other places?" That is one of the most commonly asked questions I receive from both the media and the general public. A few years back, the national media picked up on the fact that some group had ranked Wisconsin second in the country when it came to UFO reports. With such a high ranking, it makes perfect sense that we would also have three self-proclaimed "UFO Capitols of the World" located in the state (Bellville, Dundee, and Elmwood). Skeptics like to blame all UFO sightings on the media and Hollywood, stating that shows like the X-Files and Unsolved Mysteries, along with movies like Independence Day and Close Encounters, fool the public into believing they have seen UFOs. This school of thought loses some of its weight when you start to research Wisconsin's long history of UFO sightings. In 1870, a strange light hovered over Milwaukee. In 1895, a 10-foot red ball of light hung over the skies of Green Bay. In 1903, the people of Appleton witnessed a floating airship pass by. In 1908, a flaming sword lit up the sky around Saratoga. The list of these mysterious sightings is almost endless, and they occurred long before E.T. was ruling the box office. Every year, the UFO Wisconsin website is flooded with credible UFO reports from all over the state. The website has hundreds of UFO reports for you to check out…yet no matter how hard you try, I doubt you will find a UFO account as interesting and unusual as this one.

Investigation Log:

By all accounts, Joe Simonton was an upstanding resident who enjoyed a good reputation throughout the Eagle River area. Every year the 60-year-old (listed as 55 in some articles) plumber even dressed up as Santa Claus for the Chamber of Commerce. With such a good standing, it was with great hesitation that Simonton told the world of his story.

Just before noon on Tuesday April 18, 1961, Joe Simonton heard a bizarre noise on his rural chicken farm while he was enjoying a late lunch. Simonton strolled out to check on the disturbance, when a saucer appeared in his back yard. The strange-looking saucer was about 12 feet from top to bottom and approximately 30 feet in diameter. The outside of the saucer was a gleaming silver that was said to be brighter than chrome. The *Stevens Point Daily Journal* reported that instead of landing, the object "appeared to hover over the ground." Simonton could see that it had exhaust pipes that were six to seven inches in diameter.

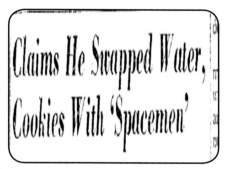

Newspapers around the country reported on Simonton's bizarre encounter.

As Simonton watched the ship hover, a hatch opened and a black-uniformed man popped out of the craft and held up a silvery looking jug, non-verbally (ESP perhaps) indicating to Simonton that it was to be filled with water. Simonton was able to look into the saucer far enough to see that the inside was dull black and he could make out some type of instrument panels. Also inside the ship were two other similarly dressed figures. The *Eau Claire Daily Telegram* wrote, "All the men were about five feet tall and weighed about 125 pounds. They were smooth shaven." Simonton also recalled that the men were Italian looking. He could see that one of the men appeared to be cooking pancakes over a flameless cooking contraption. Not one word was spoken to Simonton, nor did the men speak to each other. Simonton simply took the empty jug and set off to fill it with water. When he returned, he handed it to the man who had remained outside with the ship. In an assumed measure of appreciation for the water, one of the inside men handed Simonton three pancake shaped cakes. With the odd barter completed, the outside man grabbed the jug and re-entered the craft to the closing of the hatch. The *Oshkosh Daily Northwestern* wrote that the ship "flew off at a 45 degree angle with a swoosh that bowed near-by pine trees." Amazingly, the ship disappeared from sight within two seconds.

After the sighting, Simonton was left with the three peculiar pancakes. For the most part, these odd alien cakes looked a lot like poorly shaped regular pancakes. The cakes measured about 3 to 4 inches in diameter, one-eighth inch thick, and were perforated with little holes. With his curiosity getting the better of him, Simonton ate one of the cakes. "It tasted like cardboard," he told the Associated Press. The other two cakes were given to Vilas County Judge Frank Carter, who was an avid UFO enthusiast. Carter sent the cakes to the National Investigations Committee on Aerial Phenomena (NICAP) for testing. Initially, the committee expressed doubt as to the validly of Simonton's story and refused to analyze the cakes. Later, noted UFO researcher Dr. J. Allen Hynek had the cakes analyzed. The tests showed that the cakes were simply made out of flour, sugar, and grease. Many conspiracy theorists believe that the real findings of the cakes were classified and the more mundane report was the one given out.

Immediately after the news broke of the sighting, Simonton was inundated with calls and letters from others who told him of their

CASE 12- ALIENS BRING PANCAKES

own UFO experiences. Judge Carter told the *Capital Times* that "he was convinced Simonton actually saw the 'saucernauts,' because he was unable to think of any way in which Simonton could profit if the story were a hoax." Actually, the contrary was true, as the *Pacific Stars and Stripes* quoted Simonton, "I haven't been able to work for three weeks now and I'm going to have to start making some money." Others jumped to the defense of Simonton. District Attorney Calvin Burton told the *Sheboygan Press* that Simonton "sounded sincere," and added that he "had a good reputation in the community." Dan Satran, the Eagle River newspaper editor, told the *Oshkosh Daily Northwestern* that Simonton "is regarded by the town as a very trustworthy man…people aren't challenging the story."

Joe Simonton holds one of the space cakes the aliens gave him.

Others provided a different type of corroboration to Simonton's story with their own UFO sightings. While Simonton was busy interacting with the strange suited men, Savino Borgo was driving along on Highway 70. When he got about a mile from Simonton's farm, Borgo spotted a strange saucer-shaped craft in the sky. Other sightings of bizarre crafts in the area began to surface as well. The *Sheboygan Press* wrote, "Two other men, Gibb Sanborn, manager of the Wisconsin State Employment service office at Eagle River, and Jack Long, a Boulder Junction merchant, said they had also sighted saucers recently."

On April 27, the Lorbetske family noticed something strange in the sky.

According to the *Stevens Point Daily Journal*, "All reported the object as flying quite high, extremely fast, bright and shiny and circular." The family called the report into the Oneida County Sheriff. It is interesting to note that the Lortbtske farm was located in the same general area as Joe Simonton's farm. Speaking with the Oneida County Sheriff Department, I found out that no files from 1961 currently exist. I am still amazed that throughout the U.S., files only 40 or 50 years old might as well be 2,000 years old, because so many places simply had them destroyed. In January of 2011, I decided to try and locate the witnesses themselves. Unfortunately, Joe Simonton is deceased, as were a few other witnesses. However, I was able to track down and speak with Brent Lorbetske who, nearly 50 years after his sighting, still could recall the unusual incident. The sighting took place at the Lortbtske farm during the summer of 1961, when 20-year-old Brent and his friend Tom (now deceased) were just hanging out and talking in Tom's car. The car was parked facing east between the house and barn when Brent noticed a "weird looking plane" in the sky slowly moving from north to south. The men watched the object float across the sky for around 10 seconds before they got out of the car for a better look. Outside they could make out that the object looked like "two pie plates put together." Brent was so excited that he darted into his house and pleaded with his mother to come out and see the weird plane. His mother took one look into the sky and said, "That is no airplane," as the three of them "gazed in awe" of the object. Brent estimated that the silver object was 1 or 2 miles away from the farm, flying at an altitude of approximately ½ mile. As they watched the object slowly travel across the sky, they noticed that it made no noise whatsoever. Finally, after observing the object for several minutes, it had traveled out of their sight. The family reported their sighting to the local Sheriff in hopes of finding some answers.

CASE 12- ALIENS BRING PANCAKES

Talking with Brent all these years later, I found him to have a very balanced approach to his sighting. He told me that he would "never suggest for a minute that the object was from another planet," yet he "wouldn't completely dismiss it either." It was refreshing to speak with Brent since he keeps a healthy, open mind regarding all of the possible explanations of his sighting. He still considers the object he saw a "UFO"…meaning that to him it still remains unidentified.

WISCONSIN ROAD GUIDE TO MYSTERIOUS CREATURES

Alien Abduction in Bloomer

Where To Encounter It:

Back roads and wooded areas
Bloomer, WI

Directions:

Due to the sensitive nature of the following information, the exact location where the woman and her family live has been excluded. The best bet for any legend hunter is to patrol the back roads of Bloomer at night while sky gazing.

CASE 13 – ALIEN ABDUCTION IN BLOOMER

Author's Note – To protect the identity of the woman and her family, all names of witnesses have been changed. Several of the investigators involved with this case have had their names omitted as well.

Creature Lore:

Out of all the bizarre creatures featured in this guide, the possibility of extraterrestrial biological entities (aliens) interacting with humans is by far one of the most compelling. For decades researchers, philosophers, physicists, and people of faith have debated what the ramifications that the existence of an otherworldly being would have on us. For most people, this is just an intellectual experiment, but for many others, it is an all too terrifying reality. In the United States alone, millions of people have professed a belief that they have been abducted against their will by some sort of alien being. When we think of these events taking place, we often imagine that they occur in other locations, far away from our daily lives. Yet, for one rural Bloomer family, their encounters with alien beings took place right in their own backyard.

History of Lore:

Mary and her family lived quietly in a comfortable home on the outskirts of Bloomer. In 1997, Mary contacted the Minnesota chapter of the Mutual UFO Network (MUFON), who then put her in contact with a research colleague of mine named John Carpenter. Carpenter met with Mary after a lecture he had given in Eau Claire, and after the meeting, Minnesota researcher Craig Lang joined the investigation with us. Although the woman reached out to us in 1997, we would all soon discover that Mary's bizarre encounters had been taking place long before that.

Mary's first memory of something not quite right took place while she was still in high school during the late 1970s. In her dream, Mary was awoken by a strange, hairy man who "looked like some kind of solider, but he was not human." Not knowing how, Mary had a strong feeling that she knew who this creature was and that he was visiting her in order to say goodbye. In her dream, Mary expressed great sadness that the creature was leaving. When she awoke the next morning, Mary gave the odd dream little thought. It wasn't until much later that Mary would start to piece together all of her puzzling events.

Mary's drawing of the creature that appeared at her bedside.

During her high school days, Mary was dating a young man named Bob (now her husband). One Friday evening back in 1976 or '77, Bob picked Mary up to go out for some evening trout fishing. While out at the water, time quickly passed and the couple soon found themselves extremely sleepy. Even though they were only a few miles from home, for some odd reason the couple decided to camp

CASE 13 – ALIEN ABDUCTION IN BLOOMER

overnight in their car. Bob was sprawled out in the front seat, while Mary quickly fell asleep in the back. Their sleep came to a sudden end when, sometime during the night, Bob awoke to find his car shaking violently, as though someone was lifting it from the outside. A bit confused, Bob assumed some prankster was outside playing a trick on them, but when he looked out the window to get a better view, he saw an extremely bright light shining down on the car from above. Bob remembered that the lights were bright, changed colors, and seemed to be flashing. To matters even more strange, whatever was causing the lights and shaking was emitting absolutely no noise. Bob reported that the shaking went on for approximately one minute, during which he was so terrified that he was physically unable to move. Then the lights suddenly vanished, and the car stopped moving. Nearly in a state of panic, Bob noticed that Mary had somehow slept through the entire event. Bob scrambled to wake Mary up and explained that something was outside shaking the car and that he wanted to leave the area immediately. Without even waiting for Mary's response, Bob started the car and the couple tore off toward home.

Investigation Log:

Although the previous events rang out as being weird and unusual, they still fell into the category of possibly being explained away. Unfortunately for Mary, the next accounts are anything but explainable.

In November of 1996, Mary had an experience that she described as "very frightening and disturbing." Late one night, Mary was sound asleep in her bed when she was jolted awake by something that was being pressed against her left shoulder. She could sense that someone was standing there beside her, but before she could even look, she was grabbed by her feet and flipped onto her stomach. Trying to wrap her head around what was taking place Mary noticed that she had completely lost control of her body. Mary tried to explain her inability to struggle by saying, "I couldn't move, like I was frozen." Mary was then face down on top of her husband, who she could see was still in a deep sleep and unaware of the terror his wife was experiencing. Mary desperately tried to scream or scratch at her husband as she was slowly being pulled from the bed by some unseen force. Halfway out of the bed, Mary's world turned black and the next thing she remembered she was standing in her kitchen staring at a peculiar light that was shining in from the backyard. Mary also noticed that the windows had been opened funny and a slight breeze was blowing though the curtains. Still feeling like she was trapped in some wicked dream, Mary remembered "being told I was tired and should go back to bed," which is exactly what she did. The next morning, Mary discovered three unusual dots on her left toe that were shaped like a triangle. Years later, Mary would end up having surgery on her left shoulder (where something pushed against her in bed) to restore proper blood flow.

On another occasion, Mary described a truly baffling spotting of some unknown creature. She was working nights, and one evening when she left for work she spotted "a very strange bird" in her driveway. She only caught a quick glimpse of the creature, because it flew off so fast. Mary's description of the creature is as follows: "It was white and about 3 feet tall or so, could've been 4 feet. It was not a crane because it had a bigger body and the neck was not long like a crane, and the head was bigger – not like a bird." As Mary got into her vehicle and headed off to work, the creature flew right in front of her, so close, in fact, that its feet hit her windshield. Mary stated, "I thought I must have killed it and slowed down to look, but it just flew off." It is interesting to note that later, even Mary doubted the original "bird" title she had given to the puzzling creature. Her description of some creature standing 3-4 feet tall

CASE 13 – ALIEN ABDUCTION IN BLOOMER

with a small neck and large head is consistent with thousands of other abductees who often remember seeing similar shaped giant creatures that are remembered as owls, squirrels, and deer—all of which match the same odd proportions that Mary described, and many of them turn out to be a type of alien dubbed "greys."

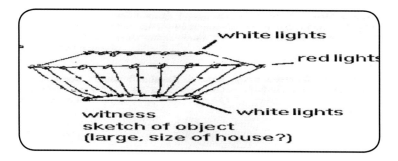

Mary's drawing of the UFO that she saw during her abduction.

Perhaps the strangest and most frightening event took place in November of 1996. It was late at night when Mary awoke from her sleep with the feeling that she had to go to the bathroom. On the way to the bathroom, she passed by the laundry room which had a large window overlooking their backyard. As she walked by, something out of the ordinary caught her attention. Moving closer to the window, she noticed a huge craft rise up from the wooded area about one-fourth of a mile north of their backyard. She could see that the craft had three rows of lights as it moved very slowly toward the house. Mary's initial reaction to the unidentified craft seemed a bit odd to us, yet it would soon make perfect sense. After seeing this object, she told us, "I stood there in awe watching it, and it suddenly dawned on me that I should lock the doors and windows, because it was heading towards our house." Mary hurriedly locked up the back door and then sprinted off toward the front, but by the time she got to it, "they were there." A strange mist had begun to drift in under the door and began to spread through the entire room. From the front window, she could see lights from a small ship that appeared to be hovering in the front yard. What happened next would haunt Mary for quite some time. She stated, "I ran to try to get the door closed, but they were already coming through it. All I recall seeing was a hand push on the door and someone saying or conveying the idea that I was acting like a foolish child and should straighten out...that I knew better than to try to lock the door...it can't keep them out anyway and that I ought to know better by now." Ignoring the warning, Mary bravely tried to push the door closed, but felt a strong force pushing it open. As the door slowly pried open, she noticed a small hand reaching around toward the inside handle. The hand slid its way around the door, and she noticed it came in a bit lower than the handle, placing it at about a child's height. Something about the hand bothered Mary. As she put it, "there weren't five fingers, and it wasn't like a human hand. It was longer and thinner." The force had pushed Mary behind the door when she blacked out. The next thing she remembered was waking up in her room the next morning.

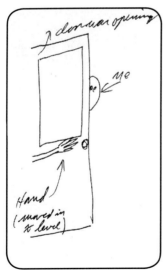

Mary's drawing of the unknown hand that forced open her front door.

Sometime after the previous events, Mary and her family discovered strange burn marks in the backyard where the UFO had been seen. The family stated that they had no idea how the strange markings appeared in their backyard. It is interesting to note that the main burn mark seems

CASE 13 – ALIEN ABDUCTION IN BLOOMER

to trail off in the same direction in which Mary remembered the craft flying away.

Mysterious burn mark that was discovered after Mary's abduction experience.

In 1998, Mary agreed to go under hypnosis with Professor (name omitted) to see if any further details of her case could be gained. It was under hypnosis that she remembered being taken from her room by three creatures that first appeared to her as floating balls of light. The creatures were approximately 4 feet tall, with large heads and strange almond eyes (similar to her bird sighting). Her description fits that of other abductees who report being taken by a type of alien dubbed the "greys." Mary could recall being floated out of her room into some sort of craft, although how she got through the entrance of the craft was unknown. Once on the craft, she could see other humans that were similarly placed on what appeared to be some type of examination table. Mary was subjected to several medical procedures in which the true purpose remains unknown. Under hypnosis, Mary began crying and stated that she was trying to grow her hair out long. When asked why, she replied that all of the humans she saw on board were completely naked, while the aliens were all fully clothed. Therefore, if she could grow her hair out long enough, the aliens would be unable to see her naked body, and she could capture some semblance of control over the situation. After the mysterious procedures were completed, Mary found herself back in her home, unaware that anything out of the ordinary had transpired.

Amazingly, after years of being visited by alien beings, removed from her home against her will, subjected to countess unknown medical tests, and mysterious markings appearing on her body, Mary still has a positive outlook on the situation. She summed up her attitude completely when she wrote us, "At first frightened by the events, I now feel endured to them, like they were a necessary part of something profound that is going on. Something that I have become a part of, whether I like it or not."

CASE 14 – MYSTERIOUS BEAST OF EAU CLAIRE

Mysterious Beast of Eau Claire

Where To Encounter It:

Highway 37 & Highway 53
Eau Claire, WI

Directions:

Highway 37 – Head south on Hwy 37 until you pass Hipp's Pub and Grub on your right. This is the area where the sighting took place.

Highway 53 – Head south out of town approximately 3-4 miles, and you will be in the vicinity of the sighting.

Creature Lore:

Throughout this book you will discover odd stories of people seeing werewolves, hellhounds, and even Bigfoot, yet this next creature doesn't seem to easily fit into any one specific category. Late at night a large unknown beast-like creature(s) has been spotted roaming the rural roadsides of Eau Claire's country highways. The beast has been spotted on several different nights and at several different locations, leading some to believe that this is not some lone creature. Just how many of these creatures are out there is still unknown and nearly impossible to predict. But what you will soon discover is that no matter how many of these creatures there are, they have been terrorizing Eau Claire for much longer than originally thought.

History of Lore:

After the recent sightings of the strange creature, I started to dig though old newspaper accounts and discovered that perhaps this creature was not new to the area. In fact, reports of the unknown creature dated back over 100 years. In March of 1908, the *La Crosse Tribune* ran an article titled "Beast Causes Terror." The article reported that a "wild beast" had been terrorizing residents in Eau Claire County. Adding additional fear to an already watchful community were the complaints from local farmers who claimed that some night-stalking creature had devoured their sheep and calves. On several occasions farmers would awake to find that some of their livestock had been torn to shreds by a vicious predator. While bloody animal carcasses were one thing, matters got even more disturbing when the story broke that the creature had quietly stalked behind a farmer's young son as he was making his way home. Luckily no human victims were reported during the

CASE 14 – MYSTERIOUS BEAST OF EAU CLAIRE

scare, and slowly over the years the terror of the beast somewhat subsided...that is until recent sightings re-vamped the legend.

Investigation Log:

The City of Eau Claire is quite deceptive; with over 65,000 residents, it appears as a bustling sprawling city, yet travel only a couple of miles from downtown, and

> **BEAST CAUSES TERROR**
>
> EAU CLAIRE, Wis., March 19.— A wild beast said to be a panther, has been terrorizing residents in the southwestern part of Eau Claire

The 1908 La Crosse Tribune article that spread fear throughout the area.

the landscape quickly turns very rural. It is there on the old rural highways that an unknown beast prowls the countryside.

In 2001, I was contacted by a woman who was a bit shaken up by an odd late night experience. The woman was employed as a nurse at Sacred Heart Hospital in Eau Claire. Her nightly shift ended at 11pm, and after work she always headed off for her home, which was a bit of a ways out in the country. The dark drive home through the country necessitated that the woman stayed ever vigilant about avoiding deer and other various creatures that could end up as roadkill. The woman didn't really mind the commute, and she saw it as an opportunity to de-escalate from a stressful shift. Most drives were uneventful, and slowly the commute became her standard nightly routine. However, little did she know that her uneventful quiet routine was about to be shattered. On what seemed like just another regular drive home, the woman was making her way south down Highway 37 when something odd caught the attention of her eye. Instinctively, she slowed down to grab a glimpse of what she immediately thought was an extremely large dog. As her vehicle slowed, the real shape of the creature emerged. Crouching off to the side of the road was a large, heavily-muscled creature whose size was similar to a large bear, yet its shape was more like that of a dog, wolf, or panther. The creature was perched on all fours and cast an intimidating presence with it shimmering black skin. The woman didn't dwell too long on the creature's bizarre shape because something else had shifted her attention, and it is what the woman saw next that would give her nightmares.

It was approximately 11:30pm, which meant that the country sky was extremely dark. This fact made it even easier for the woman to notice that the mysterious creature lurking on the side of the road had glowing red eyes that brightly pierced through the dark of night. The woman was now highly frightened, yet at the same time she inextricably felt almost mesmerized by the creature's blazing gaze. The glowing red that showcased the eyes also seemed to be emanating from the beast's mouth as well. Having lived in the country for many years the woman was well-versed in Wisconsin animals, yet it was impossible for her to say what this beast was. Disbelieving what she was seeing, and sensing the creature was out to cause her great bodily harm, the frightened woman hit the gas and torn off toward home. During our follow-up interviews, the woman confided that while she normally considered herself a pretty brave person, on the night of her sighting she had quickly lost of control over her fear. Once she reached the safety of her home, the woman eventually calmed down, and soon began to regret that she hadn't stayed around longer to better observe the creature.

There are several interesting points to this bizarre sighting. First, the woman firmly believed that whatever she had spotted that night was not a flesh-in-blood creature. On the contrary, the woman was convinced that the creature was somehow supernatural in nature. While the whole sighting only lasted a few seconds, the woman feared that if she had stayed any longer, the creature would have killed her. It is also interesting to point out the

CASE 14 – MYSTERIOUS BEAST OF EAU CLAIRE

glowing red eyes and mouth of the creature is similar to witnesses' descriptions of Chupacabras, hellhounds, and Mothman sightings. After interviewing the witness, I scoured the area of the sighting looking for any clues to the identification of the animal. Hoping to discover some paw prints, hair, or even scat, I unfortunately left the area empty handed. Whatever was prowling the area had left little evidence of its presence. What this woman encountered I do not know, but one thing that I do know is that she wasn't the only one who saw this creature.

For over 100 years this creature has been prowling the back roads of Eau Claire.

Nearly one year after collecting the abovementioned story, I received another eerily similar experience with what I was now calling the Eau Claire Beast. The second witness was an employee of an Eau Claire TV station who worked on producing the evening news. Working the 10 o'clock newscast meant that she left work around 11pm each night. The woman and her husband owned a nice place just outside of the city off of Highway 53. One evening after work, the woman was heading south out of town on Highway 53 when her headlights flashed against the outline of some creature positioned on the side of the road. Slowing down to avoid any possibly collision, the woman was amazed to see a very large panther-like creature off in the gully. The woman thought that it had to be a bear, yet it was so muscular, the body type didn't quite fit. Perhaps the woman's headlights startled the beast, because it quickly darted for the safety of the brush. Initially the woman thought little of her encounter; it wasn't until she arrived home that the bizarreness of it set in, and she decided to report her experience.

Immediately after comparing each experience I was struck by the uncanny similarities that both sightings shared. Both witnesses were women. Both sightings had taken place at approximately 11:30pm, and in both the cases the creature was spotted near the main road of a rural area. The only main difference was the fact that the creature's glowing red eyes and mouth were absent from the second sighting. These sightings left me with more questions than answers. Were these two bizarre creatures one in the same, or are there several of these unknown creatures prowling the countryside? What actually were these mysterious creatures? Questions like these remain unanswered, and even though the first reports started in the early 1900s, we still remain baffled by them today. Until one is captured or killed, we may never know what kind of being the creature really is.

CASE 15 – THE HELLHOUNDS OF MERIDEAN

The Hellhounds of Meridean

Where To Encounter It:

Meridean Boat Landing
Elk Mound, WI

Directions:

From Eau Claire, take Highway 37 south (west) and follow it for a bit until you veer right at the first fork (Wisconsin Trunk 85). Turn right on County Rd. H., then turn right on 240th Ave. which will stop/stagger on 930th Ave. Turn right, and then quickly pick up 240th Ave. again by turning left, and follow it as you pass over the small bridge. A bit down the road, the boat landing will be on your left hand side – directly along the river right before the steep hill.

Creature Lore:

Perhaps no other creature featured in this book was as feared and dreaded throughout history as hellhounds have been. Their appearance alone is enough to frighten even the most hardened legend tripper. The most common description of the hellhound is that of a large, heavily-muscled black dog with glowing red or green eyes that is also equipped with vicious razor sharp claws and teeth. Hellhounds caused great trepidation among villagers who tried to avoid them at all costs, because the creatures were thought to roam the night while conducting the Devil's bidding. Those unfortunate souls who were unlucky enough to encounter a hellhound rarely survived to share their experience with others.

I spent a good amount of time in Central America, tracking down reports and legends of hellhounds. While in Belize, villagers vehemently warned us not to stay out after dark because if we did not return by sundown, it would be too dangerous—we might encounter one of their hellhounds, called El Cadejos. They warned that if a negro (black) cadejo spotted you, it would supernaturally connect with you and slowly drain away of all your energy; unless you could locate a powerful shaman or bush doctor, you would be dead within a week. Even though the majority of cadejo sightings involved a negro creature, villagers also told us of several blanco (white) colored beasts as well. Strangely, the blanco colored creatures were thought to be friendly protectors that would often lead disoriented or drunken wanderers safely back to the village.

History of Lore:

If you believe all the legends, the former island village of Meridean has a long history of tragedy, sorrow, and unexplained events. There are numerous stories of how the island received its name,

CASE 15 – THE HELLHOUNDS OF MERIDEAN

and nearly all of the tales involve a young girl named Mary Dean, who met her maker while passing by the island. While the actual cause of Mary's death remains unknown, several eerie versions are often spun.

The more mundane of the various stories tells of Mary and her mother taking a steamboat trip along the river. During the trip, Mary was a big hit with her fellow passengers until she was stricken with an unknown illness. As her condition quickly worsened, the boat pulled up to the island and Mary was taken ashore. Shortly upon arriving on the island, death paid Mary a visit, and she succumbed to her illness. The passengers joined in with Mary's mother and insisted that Mary receive a proper funeral and burial. After a make shift service on the island, Mary's body was laid to rest under a tree. The island was then dubbed Meridean in honor of young Mary's memory.

In 1895, the *Eau Claire Weekly Leader* wrote of another version of Mary's death, claiming "Mary Dean, and the story is, a beautiful maiden traveling in company with a Presbyterian minister and his wife, Mr. and Mrs. Hunter. They were all missionaries and came here in the year 'one' to benefit the savages. Mary fell sick coming up on a keel boat, and she died where the big mill stood, 1839 or 1840."

A third and more macabre version was recounted in a 1923 article of the *Eau Claire Leader*. This version states Mary was a cook on one of the many steamboats that operated throughout the area. Instead of falling ill, the young Mary got a little too close to the edge of the boat, lost her balance, and plummeted into the chilly river where, after quite a struggle and suffering, she finally met her watery grave.

After the death of Mary, the place became known as Mary Dean Slough and eventually became Meridean, yet the stories of the cursed place were just beginning. Almost immediately after Mary's death, strange events began to take place, and Meridean gained a reputation of being a cursed island. In order to reach the island, residents and visitors had to use the ferry service that departed from both sides of the river. It is alleged that soon after Mary died, several operating ferries sank under mysterious circumstances.

For years, the island operated as a small thriving community. Much of Meridean's history remains unknown, and one can only guess at the number of homes and businesses that at one time stood on the island. The same 1923 *Eau Claire Leader* article told of the town being made up of several sawmills, a garage, post office, creamery, bank, Norwegian Lutheran church, school, and a well-stocked mercantile. It is believed that at one point over 100 residents called the island home. One sinister legend tells of a doctor on the island who owned several large dogs. These dogs were considered part of the doctor's family until they snapped and viscously tore apart one of the doctor's own children. The killers had to be put to death, and thus began the origin of the hellhounds that haunt the old ferry boat landing.

Investigation Log:

Due to the close proximity to the widely-known haunted town of Caryville, the boat landing of Meridean receives a lot of traffic from curious visitors. Not to be out done by its haunted neighbor, the boat landing comes with its own ghost story. Not only have people seen the ghostly image of a young woman out in the middle of the river, many who visit on quiet nights will experience the ghost of Mary Dean, whose spirit acts like a siren out in the water, enticing helpers with cries of desperation and panic. However, this is one ghost best left alone, as teenagers warn each other that if anyone goes in to save Mary Dean, they will never return and will be doomed to spend eternity in the dark churning waters of the river.

CASE 15 – THE HELLHOUNDS OF MERIDEAN

The feared hellhound of Meridean.

There is more to fear at the old boat landing than that of an angry ghost, as deadly hellhounds also patrol the area in search of victims. One of the older stories I was able to track down was said to have taken place nearly 60 years ago. A parked truck was found down at the boat landing of Meridean. It was believed that two young kids who had gone down to the area and parked their vehicle there were brutally torn apart by some fierce wild beast. When police looked inside the vehicle, they discovered blood splattered all over the interior, but the bodies of the victims were missing. Further analysis uncovered clumps of hair from some unidentified animal, and the bodies of the youngsters were never found. Although this makes for a troublingly good story, I have yet to find any evidence of this case.

Not everyone who believes they have encountered a hellhound at the boat landing actually sees it. I have talked with a lot of people, who while out at the boat landing, hear something big rustling in the woods. Usually this in itself is not alarming, due to the remoteness of the area, which is filled with deer and possibly even a few bears. It is not until witnesses hear horrifying growling and snarling coming from the woods that they realize the animal is not a deer.

WISCONSIN ROAD GUIDE TO MYSTERIOUS CREATURES

I received a report from a woman who had a sighting of something very strange trotting down the road as it passed the boat landing. The event took place in 2005 when a woman and her mother took a legend trip out to the boat landing. It was just after 10pm and the night air had cooled the temperature down to the mid 50s. The night was dry, and the sky was clear when the women noticed some type of animal loping along the road. Getting a closer look, the women were shocked to see that running down the road was what appeared to be a white wolf. This was no ordinary wolf, as the women reported that it was completely transparent; they could see right through it.

I was in the middle of a book signing in Stevens Point when a gentleman approached me and asked if I had ever heard of hellhounds near the boat landing of Meridean. The man was a big burly biker guy, the exact type of guy that wouldn't get scared by anything. He told me that one day during a motorcycle ride near Eau Claire, he and a couple of his friends decided to take their bikes out to see the ghost of Mary Dean. It was just about dusk as the small group motored in to the area of the boat landing. Immediately they spotted several large black dogs roaming near the boat landing. Fearing that the dogs were out to harm them, the bikers quickly decided to scurry out of the area as fast as they could. When I asked him why he thought the creatures were hellhounds and not just plain wild dogs, the now visibly shaken man stated that several things about these hellish canines convinced him that they were not normal dogs. On their arrival, the bikers were able to see that the dogs appeared to be nearly transparent—the group could almost see right through them. The second thing that freaked them out was the fact that the group exited the area at a quick pace, but the hellhounds had no problem keeping up with them, no matter how fast they went. With a gruesome looking hellhound running right next to him, the

CASE 15 – THE HELLHOUNDS OF MERIDEAN

man kicked out his foot and attempted to hit the ferocious dog, yet much to his surprise, his foot simply went right through the creature. This aggressive action seemed to work, because after the kick, the dogs simply disappeared into the night. The group was so shook up about the incidence that they did not stop riding until the hit the safety of Chippewa Falls (about 30 miles away).

During one of my investigations of Meridean, I had arrived at the boat landing with my colleague Terry Fisk just as the sun was setting and darkness was beginning to creep in. As we started to discuss the basis of the numerous legends, the night air was pierced by a loud, strange, animal-like sound coming from the island. We rushed to the car to grab some recording equipment, hoping that the odd sound would repeat itself. The mysterious noise we heard was a bit hard to describe. The confusing aspect of it was that it sounded as though it was part-human / part-animal, yet we were unable to match it to any locally known animal. Unfortunately for us, the island remained deadly quiet for the rest of the investigation, and we never captured a recording of the unusual sound.

WISCONSIN ROAD GUIDE TO MYSTERIOUS CREATURES

The Bear-Wolf Beast of Holy Hill

Where To Encounter It:

Outside the entrance of Holy Hill on Highway 167
Hubertus, WI

Directions:

From Hubertus, head west on Highway 167. When you are outside the entrance of Holy Hill, you will see the street sign for Troll Hill Road on your right (across the road from the entrance). This is where the sighting took place.

CASE 16 – THE BEAR-WOLF BEAST OF HOLY HILL

Creature Lore:

The world is full of creatures that don't easily fall into any recognizable category. While the more infamous monsters like Bigfoot and Nessie of Loch Ness get the majority of the attention, the real weirdness comes with those creatures that are so bizarre that they defy logic. The bear-wolf-type creature looks as if it combines the physical characteristics of both the Bigfoot and the werewolf, while maintaining its own uniqueness that separates it from all other beings. In her book, *Hunting the American Werewolf*, researcher Linda Godfrey tells of dozens of accounts of encounters with these seemingly hybrid bear-wolf creatures. Amid his various lectures and presentations, Wisconsin-based paranormal researcher and folklorist Todd Roll has also collected several odd tales from witnesses who have seen a similar bear-wolf-type creature prowling the countryside of Wisconsin.

The early Native American tribes of Wisconsin held strong beliefs in many supernatural creatures—including the Bigfoot, wendigo, and sasquatch—making it possible that sightings of a bear-wolf creature were simply tossed in with the other long-established creatures. The early days of Wisconsin also saw the rise of what were known as "wild man" sightings. These wild man reports ran the gamut when it came to their descriptions. Most of the wild men fell into one of two categories. First were the men who were simply thought to be feral-looking old hermits that had spent years living alone in the woods. The second, more supernatural type, were said to be extremely tall and heavily-muscled beings whose bodies were covered in long, thick, matted-down fur. It is entirely possible that several of these wild men also fit into the bear-wolf category.

History of Lore:

Since its beginning, Holy Hill has been steeped in mystery. The place has long been considered a spiritual hotbed and quickly gained a reputation as a place where miracles occur. In 1903, the *Eau Claire Weekly Telegram* ran the article "Hill Not Holy." The article tells of several clergymen who believed that Holy Hill "is misnamed and that none of the marvelous and miraculous cures claimed to have been made at the shrine have stood the test of investigation."

Investigation Log:

Having spent several years removing roadkill for Washington County, Steve Krueger thought he had seen it all. His nightly route brought him the opportunity to come in contact with many nocturnal critters. Krueger's familiarity with Wisconsin's wildlife took a drastic change during the late night hours of November 9, 2006. His story was covered extensively in both the local and national media, many of which erroneously reported what had happened. So, what actually did happen on that dark and quiet night? To find out, I decided to interview Krueger, who informed me that the encounter went like this. It was around 1:30am on the night/morning of November 9th and he was beginning his usual rounds and listening to the radio when he spotted a small deer lying on the side of the road. The deer wasn't on his list of pickups, meaning that it probably had been freshly killed. Krueger turned on the flashing orange beacon lights positioned on the top of his truck and quickly pulled to the side of the road. He got out of the truck to retrieve the carcass, which turned out to be a small doe that only weighed 70-80 pounds which allowed him to forgo the metal ramp which was used for heavier animals. With the tailgate down, he had no trouble hoisting the deer into the well-lit truck bed. Leaving the

CASE 16 – THE BEAR-WOLF BEAST OF HOLY HILL

deer in the back, Krueger walked back into the cab to complete the paperwork and tag needed to register the new kill. As he was filling out the paperwork, he felt the truck shake but paid little attention to it, thinking it was the wind. Then the truck shook again, and this time it wasn't the wind. Curious, Krueger looked into his rearview mirror and was shocked to see a large unknown creature leaning into the truck bed. Although only the upper half of the beast was visible, he knew it was big and very wide. He told me the creature was "the size of a large bear, but with a wolf's head." Whatever the beast was, it intentions seemed clear; Krueger could see that it "had its arm around the leg of the deer." Not knowing what type of creature he was dealing with, he threw the truck into drive and tore off. In the process he heard the sound of one of his ramps hitting the pavement. Most likely the deer's foot had gotten tangled in the ramp, and when the creature tugged the deer from the truck, the ramp came with it.

Road signs marking the spot where the bear-wolf encounter took place.

After driving for a minute, Krueger turned around and drove back to retrieve the fallen ramp. Still a bit fearful that the creature might be lurking in the area, he hesitantly got out and searched the area for his ramp, which had mysteriously gone missing. With neither the creature nor the ramp anywhere in sight, Krueger climbed back into the truck and continued on his way. As he continued on his route, his mind was racing with the possibilities of what had just transpired. Noting that no other vehicles had passed by him while he was on the road, it was unlikely that someone else had removed the deer and ramp. He also feared that the creature might be aggressive. If it was brave enough to snatch a deer right from the back of his truck, than what else was it capable of? With this in mind, at approximately 4am, Krueger decided to drive to the Sheriff's office and report his encounter. He was adamant that what he saw was not a Bigfoot and took great care in not using the word in his report. The department sent out a couple of deputies, but according to their report they were "unable to locate any sign of the ramp, any sign that there might have been an animal dropped on the pavement, nor was there any sign of any other type of creature dragging a deer carcass away from the roadway."

CASE 16 – THE BEAR-WOLF BEAST OF HOLY HILL

The roadside where the deer carcass was grabbed.

So, if the creature Krueger encountered wasn't a Bigfoot, what in the heck was it? Keep in mind that he only viewed the beast for approximately five seconds, but it was long enough for him to make out some extremely bizarre details. If the creature made any noise in its approach, Krueger did not hear it over the blare of the radio. From what he saw, he estimated that the creature was 6-7 feet in height and was fully covered in dark, two-inch-long fur. Although the body was the size of a big bear, it was shaped quite differently and was very wide. With a longer muzzle and pointed triangle shaped ears, the head of the creature resembled that of a wolf with long arms. Having spent several years picking up rotting corpses, he was unable to discern if the creature gave off any odor. When I spoke with Krueger in 2011, he was still as baffled by the incident as he was back in 2006.

Whatever the bear-wolf creature is, it does not seem to fear humans.

Immediately after the event took place media outlets from all over the country covered the story—many of them inaccurately claiming that Steve had encountered a Bigfoot. However, the word "Bigfoot" does not appear anywhere in the Sheriff's Department report. In an all too common reaction to paranormal events, skeptics immediately sought to tarnish the reputation of the witness while also trying to cast doubt on the actual sighting. Yet in his report, Deputy Stolz wrote, "Steve Krueger showed no signs of deceptive behavior when I was asking his questions, and did not appear to have made up the story." Krueger informed me that so much attention had been cast on his sighting that he wished he would have just kept his mouth shut and never reported his encounter. Fortunately for us legend trippers, he did report his sighting and provided us with a great starting point in finding the Bear-Wolf of Holy Hill…just make sure to keep a close eye on your carcasses.

CASE 17 – THE BEAST OF BRAY ROAD

The Beast of Bray Road

Where To Encounter It:

Bray Road and Walworth County
Elkhorn, WI

The property off of Bray Road is private—Please view from the road

Directions:

From Elkhorn, travel east on Highway 11 for approximately 4 miles; Bray Road will be on your right. You can then follow Bray Road to the west for its entire 4 miles.

Creature Lore:

Wisconsin is full of supernatural creatures, but none have come close to achieving the level of notoriety of the Beast of Bray Road. Numerous books, role-playing games, and even a movie have propelled the creature up to the familiarity of the Jersey Devil, Mothman, and Dover Demon. What is this bipedal werewolf-looking creature doing prowling the back roads and wooded areas of Wisconsin? And why does it use the short, rural Bray Road as its main stomping grounds?

History of Lore:

One of the oldest sightings collected by researcher Linda Godfrey is recounted in her co-authored book, *Weird Wisconsin*. It was in 1936 when a Jefferson County security watchman thought he spotted something moving around in the darkness directly behind his work building. As he squinted to get a better look, it appeared as though some type of creature was digging around in an old Native American burial mound. Without much thought, the man just assumed the creature was merely a lone dog searching for a meal. But when he focused his flashlight on the supposed canine, he quickly realized that the animal was certainly no dog. Instead, the man saw a very large, shaggy creature with pointed ears and three long claws on each hand.

Sightings of the mysterious wolf-like creature continued to occur throughout the decades, but most witnesses kept what they saw to themselves, fearing that they would be ridiculed by their friends and family. Slowly, residents began to whisper to one another about the most recent sightings of the mysterious wolf-like beast. Eventually, the accumulation of sightings reached a breaking point and witnesses felt secure in reporting their bizarre experiences.

CASE 17 – THE BEAST OF BRAY ROAD

In *Hunting the American Werewolf*, Linda Godfrey included a puzzling story that occurred sometime in 1964 or 1965. Approximately one-half mile from Bray Road sat an old family farm on Bowers Road. One evening, all of the children decided to have a campout in their back yard. While playing around in the darkness with their German Shepherd, the children spotted something large and dark moving near the woods. In fact, the mysterious animal appeared to be larger than any they had ever seen before. The creature spooked them so much that they scampered to the safety and protection of their tent. While huddled inside the tent, the kids swore they heard the animal grunting and growling as it stalked its way towards them. As the animal got closer, the children heard their dog dash off toward the mysterious creature. Soon the quiet night air was shattered by the growling and yelping sounds of two animals clashing outside their tent. Unable to see what was taking place, the children could only pray for the best. When their dog returned to them with deep scratches and bloody wounds, the children assumed it had driven off the mysterious creature—hopefully for good. Their dog may have gotten off lightly, as some of my favorite Bray Road sightings are those that feature the beast holding, dragging, or consuming other animals or roadkill. In *Weird Wisconsin*, Godfrey tells of a woman who spotted the beast kneeling down near the side of the road with some type of roadkill in its arms. Others have similarly reported seeing the creature carrying, eating, and inspecting roadkill animals.

WISCONSIN ROAD GUIDE TO MYSTERIOUS CREATURES

The place where it all started---Bray Road.

In 2005, a movie about the beast aptly titled *The Beast of Bray Road* was released. The movie, directed by Leigh Scott, spent the entire 80 minutes casting Wisconsin as the home to ignorant backwoods gun-toting alcoholic hillbillies still living in the 19th century. But don't fret about the terrible portrayal of us, because the director did dedicate the movie to the great people of Wisconsin.

Investigation Log:

The Beast of Bray Road gained international attention thanks to my good friend and colleague Linda Godfrey, who has become the leading expert on the creature. What better way to find out about the beast than by asking Godfrey herself. Having worked in the same circles with her for many years, we have traded a lot of reports of the mysterious werewolf-like creatures. In 2011, I decided to officially interview her for this book.

CASE 17 – THE BEAST OF BRAY ROAD

Back in 1991, Godfrey was working as newspaper reporter in Walworth County, when she heard rumors that people were seeing what they described as a werewolf roaming the countryside of Elkhorn near Bray Road. After interviewing several of the witnesses, Godfrey completed an article on what she dubbed "The Beast of Bray Road." After the article was printed, other sightings began flowing in. Eventually, she would end up with nearly two dozen sightings from just the Bray Road area, with many more originating throughout the entire country.

What I have always deemed fascinating about these cases is general similarities of the creatures behind these sightings. In an attempt to provide the best overall description of the beast, Godfrey told me that most witnesses describe "a 5-7-foot-tall bipedal canine covered with fur that ranges from very dark brown to gray. It has a head like a wolf or German Shepherd, pointed ears, pronounced muzzle with large fangs and dog-like legs and forelimbs." Unlike many other creatures featured in this guide, the beast doesn't seem too intimidated by human interaction, as Godfrey found that "it often acts aggressively and chases vehicles and people before it runs away." Even though the beast engages in a display of aggression, Godfrey has no knowledge of anyone actually being killed or even seriously injured by the ferocious acting beast. Much to the relief of many witnesses, once the beast finishes its scare tactics it usually quickly heads for whatever cover it can find. One feature of the beast that really

Witness description of the Beast of Bray Road.

sticks out to witnesses is its ability to walk and run upright on its hind legs, just like we do.

The question of exactly what the Beast of Bray Road is still remains. Godfrey believes that the creatures are not traditional, Hollywood-style werewolves. She speculates that "they may be some unknown wolf species that has adapted to walk upright, or perhaps they are transients from some other time or dimension." In his book, *Monster Spotter's Guide to North America*, Scott Francis brings up the theory many subscribe to that the "beast is a Shunka Warakin, a wolf-like creature of Native American mythology." Others contend that the beast may be more along the lines of the creature the Native Americans called the Wendigo, or perhaps it is even somehow related to the Bigfoot. Again, these theories are only that—theories—and the true nature of these creatures remains unknown.

Being that this is a road guide, it seems only fitting that some readers would like to get a little closer to the beast than the written page allows. For those of you traveling to Bray Road with the hopes of coming face to muzzle with the beast, keep in mind that most of the sightings take place near a water source; most—but not all—occur at night; and contrary to popular myth, the beast doesn't seem too interested in adhering to any moon cycle. Linda advises that legend trippers should come prepared with flashlights, cameras, video cameras, and the knowledge that other large predators—like wolves, bears, cougars, and coyotes—also hide in the shadows.

CASE 18 – THE GNOMES OF THE DEVIL'S PUNCHBOWL

The Gnomes of the Devil's Punch Bowl

Where To Encounter It:

Devil's Punch Bowl
Menomonie, WI

Directions:

From Hwy 25 in Menomonie, head west on Cty Rd. 29. (11th Ave. W which becomes Hudson Rd). As soon as you pass over the Red Cedar River turn left on Paradise Valley Rd. Take the next left (410th St.) and follow it for approximately 3 miles; The Devil's Punchbowl will be on your left. (There will be a small, dirt parking area; you have to walk down to the punchbowl.)

WISCONSIN ROAD GUIDE TO MYSTERIOUS CREATURES

Creature Lore:

Throughout history, cultures all around the world have reported encounters with diminutive, unknown creatures. Although these creatures have been known as elves, gnomes, goblins, fairies, sprites, little people, leprechauns, and the wee folk, their general characteristics remain similar. While these beings often appear cute and harmless, they have traditionally been viewed in a more negative light. These beings are thought to possess magical powers, making them feared creatures that should not be taken lightly. Folklore is filled with tales of humans who encountered the beings, only to have their sight, hearing, or even their lives stolen by the wee folk. It was a commonly held belief that fairies would lure away trusting children, only to replace them with almost identical-looking changelings. Needless to say, it is strongly advised that those who actively seek out these beings take the following measures to ensure that you do not fall under the spell of the elves:

1. Make sure to bring an offering to leave for the fairies. This offering can be as simple as leaving a shiny rock or small treat like skittles or M&Ms to guarantee your safe travel.

2. Never be disrespectful to the area you are exploring. Traditional lore states that these creatures are often protectors of the land and tend to punish those who are foolish enough to ignore this rule.

3. A bit more on the new age side of things are the claims that horseshoes, four-leaf clovers, and bells will act as a repellent to ward off goblins.

History of Lore:

Tucked away on the very outskirts of the City of Menomonie rests The Devil's Punchbowl... a natural formation that was part of a sea

CASE 18 – THE GNOMES OF THE DEVIL'S PUNCHBOWL

deposit laid down nearly 500 million years ago. The formation was gouged out by the glaciers that passed through over 10,000 years ago. Lucky searchers have even discovered fossils in the rocks that form one of Wisconsin's most beautiful nature areas. The early Native Americans considered the area sacred and were thought to have held many ceremonies there. Years ago, the area was widely known as Black's Ravine, due to the fact that it was owned by Civil War Captain Samuel Black. As the years passed by, the land changed ownership many times, eventually ending up in the hands of the Wisconsin Farmland Conservancy of Menomonie. The area also enjoys a well-known reputation of being a place where mysterious events transpire; long before tales of the little people began to surface, the area was rife with reports of mysterious lights and belief in the mystic properties of the punchbowl's water.

Many believe that the punchbowl is a sacred area and full of mystery.

Investigation Log:

Over the past few decades, visitors looking to enjoy a peaceful day of hiking and exploring often spotted strange balls of unidentified lights hovering through the area. According to witnesses, these disembodied balls of light would repeatedly change in size, shape, and color. A few years back, I spoke with a group of teenagers who one evening decided to travel out to punchbowl to see the place for themselves. The group was parked in the small lot, where they were debating whether or not they should venture down into the punchbowl itself. While getting up the courage to exit the car, the group noticed a ball of light start to slowly float towards them. Stricken with fear, the group was helpless and could do nothing but watch as the light got closer. They went on to tell me that the light actually entered inside their car. When I asked them, "What did you do when that ball of light entered your car?" they all looked at me as though I was crazy and replied, "We got out of the car!" In the split second that it took the group to flee the car, the light had simply vanished into the night air.

One of the stranger stories associated with the punchbowl revolves around the water from the small creek that splits its way through the area. It is said that if you collect the water while it is ice cold, it will retain its temperature, regardless of the conditions that you store it in. I am puzzled by how this legend took its roots, but each year I speak with people who claim that, no matter what they did to the water, it remained ice cold.

My favorite stories originating from the Devil's Punchbowl are the tales of the area being inhabited by gnomes. Just how long these encounters have been occurring has been lost to history, but it appears as though they are gaining in frequency. Nearly ten years ago, while I was a student of the University of Wisconsin-Stout

CASE 18 – THE GNOMES OF THE DEVIL'S PUNCHBOWL

(located about four miles from the punchbowl), I was contacted by a woman who had spent a wonderful day hiking the area with her son. Growing a bit tired from their excursion, the two were just about to head up the stairs to their car when the mother stopped for one last gaze of the beautiful waterfall. She told me that what she saw next, she would never be able to forget. Standing on top of the waterfall was a 3 to 4-foot-tall gnome-like creature staring back at her. She immediately grabbed her son and asked if he could see the creature, but by the time the son had spun around to look, the creature had either disappeared into the woods or vanished into thin air. The woman was a bit shy and embarrassed about her report because she knew how it sounded, yet she was convinced that what she had witnessed was a gnome straight out of folklore. The creature was around three to four feet tall with pointed ears and traditional gnome-like features. The woman also noticed that the creature was wearing some type of odd clothing, complete with a large pointed cap. And while the experience only lasted a few seconds, the woman said it would stick with her forever.

Witness description of the creature that was spotted above the punchbowl.

A few years after receiving the abovementioned story, I got a call from a young couple who attended UW-Stout. A football player had taken his girlfriend out to the punchbowl to really scare her, to get her in the mood for Halloween. The couple started to descend the punchbowl, and when they reached the halfway mark they both heard the growl of some animal that they could not identify. At this point, the boyfriend's plan had backfired, as it was he who got scared and ran back to the parking lot. The brave young girl told me she waited there for an additional 15 minutes for the creature to make another noise or to show itself, but then she felt bad and had to go and rescue her boyfriend.

While I was in college, I spent a lot of my free time scouring the punchbowl, searching for signs of the little people. Although I always came away empty-handed, I truly got to enjoy the majestic beauty of the land. The area is truly a magical place, and I came to the conclusion that if gnomes are in fact real, the Devil's Punchbowl was the perfect place for them to live.

CASE 19 – THE ROCK TOSSING GNOMES OF HOLY CROSS ROAD

The Rock-Tossing Gnomes of Holy Cross Road

Where To Encounter It:

Holy Cross Road
Fifield, WI

Directions:

From Fifield, head south on US 13 for approximately 5 miles. Turn left on Holy Cross Road and drive forward to the train tracks. The wooded area to the right of the train tracks is the spot to throw the rock.

Creature Lore:

After long days of searching for gnomes and little people in Ireland, I would spend my expedition nights in a pub or two hoping to gather information from the locals. When I would ask where all the gnomes and little people were, they would say, "Which ones do you want to know about?" I was not used to such openness with matters concerning the paranormal, and I was thrown for a bit of culture shock. Everywhere I went residents seemed to keep an open mind about the possibility of gnomes residing in their neighborhoods. Now the next time you are in a pub in Wisconsin, just as an experiment, ask where all the gnomes hang out and see what kind of response you get. On second thought, I will save you the embarrassment and simply tell you where they hang out. If you have just read the Gnomes of The Devil's Punchbowl case then you have already learned all the necessary tricks and techniques needed to start your own gnome adventure.

History of Lore:

Holy Cross Road has been a paranormal hot spot for a long as locals can remember. One of the more fascinating rumors dates back to the early 1900s. Back during those times, the area was said to have been called Coolidge. Then, one day, the entire town simply disappeared without a trace. Research shows that the town of Coolidge did exist. It was founded in 1884 by W.H. Coolidge and owned by the Coolidge Lumber Company. It served mostly as a lumber camp, housing the company's workers and containing a few shops, a post office, and a spattering of lumber buildings. It is believed that a massive fire destroyed the town...not an unexplained disappearance.

CASE 19 – THE ROCK TOSSING GNOMES OF HOLY CROSS ROAD

Investigation Log:

I really enjoy these types of cases, because not only do you get a mysterious creature roaming the area, you get a bit of a paranormal bonus as well with the addition of the place being haunted. This tragic tale begins with a mother returning home with her small children. As their car neared the train tracks it started to sputter and rolled to a dead stop right in the middle of the tracks. Before the mother could even react, a train came crashing into the car, killing everyone inside. Now, on peaceful nights, visitors swear that they can see the spirit of the dead mother hovering near the lake, forced to spend eternity where she met her demise. The ghosts of the children have been spotted plenty of times as well, but their spirits seem to be on a mission to ensure the safety of anyone passing by. The legend is that if you stop your car in the middle of the tracks, your car will be pushed to safety by the phantom hands of the dead children who are protecting the road and prohibiting others from sharing their grisly fate.

A less specific phenomenon of the area is the overwhelming, uncomfortable feeling that overcomes those who wander through the land. Normally, non-psychic people suddenly experience the sensation that something is not right with the area…almost as though they are not wanted there. Others sense that they are not alone and feel as though they are being watched by some unseen force.

WISCONSIN ROAD GUIDE TO MYSTERIOUS CREATURES

Wooded area along the train tracks where the gnomes have been spotted.

Directly next to the train tracks is a small patch of wooded area where most of the gnome sightings have taken place. Most people visit the area at night, and when they arrive they immediately hear rustling coming from the wooded area. Thinking that it is nothing more than a common Wisconsin animal, most people are not alarmed. However, as the noises progress, their interest peeks a bit as they start to make out the black outlines of something small moving quickly among the trees. What sets these sightings apart from other gnome encounters is the apparent interaction between the witnesses and the supernatural creatures. Legend states that if you approach the wooded area and grab a rock from the train tracks and hurl it into the woods, the rock will be thrown right back at you by the gnomes who are occupying the mini forest. Several brave rock throwers have actually caught a glimpse of the gnomes

CASE 19 – THE ROCK TOSSING GNOMES OF HOLY CROSS ROAD

and report the creatures' physical characteristics to match the more popular view of gnomes…being 2-4 feet tall with pointed ears, wearing some type of odd garb as they stealthily move throughout the underbrush. The origin of the rock throwing remains unknown, but most likely it started when someone tried to rouse whatever was in the woods from its hiding place—only to have the rock thrown right back at them.

Be careful where you throw rocks because sometimes creatures throw them right back at you.

The Huldrefolk of Washington Island

Where To Encounter It:

Washington Island

Directions:

Washington Island is on the northern tip of Door County. To access the island you can take the ferry from Detroit Harbor.

The little folk are thought to inhabit the entire island.

CASE 20 – THE HULDREFOLK OF WASHINGTON ISLAND

Creature Lore:

In the United States many of our rituals, superstitions, and beliefs in the supernatural originated with our ancestors who flocked to this land so many years ago. Along with all of their worldly possessions they brought with them curious tales of curses, spirits, and mysterious creatures. These tales began being passed down through the art of oral storytelling. These beliefs were spread through the family, with each generation adding a new twist. Eventually the subjects of these tales were as real as they were in the old country. One creature that flourished among Washington Island's Icelandic newcomers was the huldrefolk.

There are numerous versions of the huldrefolk. The belief in these creatures originated in the Norse countries and while some tales compare them to gnomes, leprechauns, fairies and the like, others claim they appear as beautiful women with long flowing hair looking to lure away wandering men. If these creatures are indeed magical, as many believe, then it follows that they could just as easily live in the US as they could in Europe.

Undeveloped countryside of Washington Island.

History of Lore:

Washington Island is a wondrous, mystical place that many people feel inexplicably drawn to. The first white pioneers called the densely forested place "Potawatomi Island" in honor of the tribe of Native Americans that once occupied the land. In 1849, Amos Sanders purchased the island, and it quickly became a hotbed for Icelandic settlers. In fact, it is thought to be the oldest Icelandic settlement in the entire United States. Although the island's population was always small, its supernatural reputation was legendary. The waterways surrounding Washington Island seemed to be cursed, as evidenced by the countless ships that were sunk or lost while traveling the strip of water fearfully dubbed "Port des Mortes," or Death's Door. The most infamous of these lost ships was The Griffin, a ship that in 1679 had finished loading furs from Green Bay and set off, never to be heard from again. Legend states that on misty nights, witnesses have caught sight of an old phantom sailing vessel out at sea. The ghost ship has the appearance of a vessel that came straight from the 1600s. The more superstitious witnesses believe that the floating image is that of the long-lost Griffin.

Investigation Log:

The first researcher to tell of the gnomes of Washington Island was Geri Rider. In her book, *Ghosts of Door County*, she reported a fascinating story dating back to the 1850s. Rider wrote of a young Icelandic girl named Anna, who spent her nights sitting at the feet of her senior grandmother as the old woman spun amazing tales of the huldrefolk who were said to be hiding in the trees and meadows.

During the 1800s, living on the island was a hard life. The isolation meant that families had to become self-sufficient in order to survive. Little Anna did her part by gathering berries from the other side of

CASE 20 – THE HULDREFOLK OF WASHINGTON ISLAND

the island. Anna loved the outdoors and did not consider her chores to be work. One summer morning, Anna set off for the berry patch. Her routine was simple—she would get to the patch and pick until her bucket (and belly) was full and then proceed home. But one afternoon, Anna arrived home with her bucket only half full. When her mother inquired about the missing berries, Anna told of her exciting encounter with the huldrefolk. Anna claimed that while she was picking berries, she was approached by strangely dressed beings decked out in little shoes, tiny clothes and odd hats. Not knowing how to react, Anna offered them some of her berries, and to reward her generosity, the huldrefolk taught her several songs and dances before they retreated back to the hidden places of the island.

Outside of this story, I was unable to find any other accounts of gnomes on the island. I spoke with several volunteers of the island's archives who were all unfamiliar with the huldrefolk. I had originally traveled to Washington Island back in 2001 while conducting research for the book *The Wisconsin Road Guide to Haunted Locations*. During that expedition, we had no trouble at all tracking down odd haunted stories of the island, yet we came up short on finding any credible gnome sightings. In 2010, I decided to head back to the island in search of the huldrefolk. I brought with me fellow legend trippers Kevin Nelson, Noah Voss, and Sean Bindley. Together we scoured the island, looking for evidence and stories of the wee folk. We spoke with numerous life-long residents who had no personal encounters with gnomes, yet they expressed little surprise in hearing about the island's folklore.

The first stop on our investigation brought us to an old Norwegian Stave Church. The church is an absolutely amazing structure hidden back in the woods just off the main road. The first thing we took notice of was the strange symbols that strategically adorned each entrance of the building. Luckily for us, Kevin is an expert in witchcraft, sorcery, and the dark arts. He informed us that the symbols (The Helm of Awe) were placed there for protection. Trying to figure out just what the church needed protection from gave us the creeps. Although you could spend the entire day marveling at the structure, we were on a gnome hunt, so we headed off toward one of the best places to find locals who feel comfortable sharing odd stories...the bar.

The old Norwegian Stave Church.

We entered Nelson's Hall Bar and Grill, which is one hell of a cool place. The bar serves as the headquarters for the world renowned Bitters Club—a club which over 10,000 people a year join by bravely downing a shot of Angostura Bitters. Of course, the place also has a long history of being haunted. But outside of the ghosts, beer, and Bitters shots, the place has a wealth of island history and photos positioned throughout the building. We spoke with several

CASE 20 – THE HULDREFOLK OF WASHINGTON ISLAND

residents who were also unaware that the island was said to be inhabited by gnomes.

From Nelson's Hall we walked down along Range Line Road, where the spirit of a wandering woman named Gretchen resides. Often times with paranormal cases certain phenomena tend to be seen in the same areas. For example, many crop circle discoveries come with reports of UFOs or strange balls of light. Some reports claim that Bigfoot creatures are accompanied with will-o-wisps lights. With this knowledge, we took the chance that perhaps the spirit of Gretchen would encourage the little people to make themselves known. After having little luck on Range Line Road, we decided to move our base camp to another gnome hotspot…water.

Since we were on an island, it wasn't too hard to locate water. Part of the folklore of gnomes is that they like to reside near water. Whether it is a lake, pond, river, or stream, many encounters all happen within sight of water. Another trick to seeing gnomes is to call out for them while providing some type of offering. This may seem a bit far-fetched, but when you are dealing with the paranormal, nothing is off limits. We made several

Traditional gnome of Washington Island.

attempts to communicate with the beings and finally gathered up some candy to try and entice the hidden people. By now the day was nearing an end, and with no gnomes showing up, our next goal was to find a wooded area that looked like the perfect gnome gathering spot. We drove around the back roads of the island, searching for a suitable spot to make our night camp. Finally, after a thorough search, we decided to bunk down alongside a wooded area right near the water. If any place looked like it should have gnomes, it was where we put up night camp. We were all a bit edgy as we recognized that this would be our last chance to find the huldrefolk, because the following morning we were departing for nearby Rock Island to investigate a haunted graveyard and lighthouse. Unfortunately, the night passed uneventfully and it appeared that the hidden people of Washington Island were choosing to remain hidden. As we packed up our gear, we all vowed that we would soon launch another expedition to Washington Island…next time we would bring more candy.

CASE 21 – THE PIG MEN OF BRUSSELS

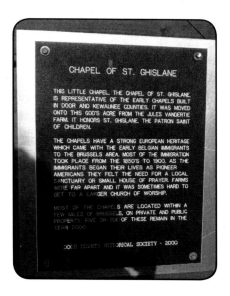

The Pig Men of Brussels

Where To Encounter It:

Saint Ghislane Chapel
Misere Road
Brussels, WI

Directions:

The town of Brussels is located in the heart of Door County.

To reach the chapel from Brussels, head south on County Road C for approximately two miles. Turn left on Co. Rd. J, then turn right on Misere Road. The chapel will be on your right side, located next to St. Michael's cemetery.

Creature Lore:

The act of cursing someone or something has been responsible for many paranormal cases around the world. Oftentimes these curses are directed towards other people, but this story illustrates that sometimes curses take on a life of their own and can have severe unintended consequences. During my nearly 20 years of paranormal research, I have encountered many paranormal stories involving pigs. I have ventured out after the phantom pigs that are thought to appear each year at the Minnesota State Fair. I was even bombarded by wild feral pigs while on a Skunk Ape expedition in the Everglades of Florida, yet I have never encountered anything even remotely resembling the pig men that are featured in this bizarre case.

History of Lore:

All around Wisconsin, nearly forgotten legends can be found by those willing to invest the time and energy necessary to resurrect them. Most of the time these intriguing legends are so obscure that they have all but disappeared, even by those directly shaped by their telling. The legend of the pig men of Brussels would have certainly remained hidden if not for the diligent research of Linda Godfrey, who discovered and shared with me the fascinating tale first recorded by Esther Menn in *Wisconsin Footsteps*.

The first Belgium settlers to the area began putting down roots in the 1850s. The town of Brussels was established in 1858 by the farming families who staked their lives on the fertile soil of the land. The exact date of the pig men curse is unknown, but most likely it originated somewhere between the years 1860-1920.

CASE 21 – THE PIG MEN OF BRUSSELS

Investigation Log:

The early settlers who arrived from Belgium brought with them the knowledge and experience needed to successfully live off of the land. Even though they were thousands of miles away from their homeland, they continued to abide by their beliefs, rituals, and religion. The new settlers looked to worship as often as they could, yet early farm life was an ever consuming occupation that often impeded on their time. In addition to the time constraints, 1800s travel was limited to horse and buggy, thus traveling the long distances to reach a neighboring church became a hardship for many people. To combat these problems, residents of the area began constructing small shines and prayer houses on the corners of their land where they could conveniently worship without the hassles of travel. Many of the chapels were designed to serve as shrines to God as appeals to help ward off illness, suffering, and to provide a bountiful crop.

Researcher and folklorist Kevin Nelson inspects the Saint Ghislane Chapel.

This legend, recorded by Esther Menn, told of a local farmer who was distraught after being left out of his rich uncle's will back in Belgium. Angry, betrayed, and looking for revenge, he put a curse on the local clergymen. Somehow during the process, the curse backfired and turned back onto the young farmer. Immediately the effects of the curse started to manifest, and odd things began happening in his home…his furniture began to dance around as phantom music could be heard floating through the homestead. Worst of all, animals began to take on the appearance of having a human face. Everywhere the farmer went, he was terrorized by pigs with human faces. These "pig men" caused the farmer such emotional turmoil that he sought out the advice of his wise older neighbor lady. The devout woman told him to put his faith in the Lord by constructing a shrine to make reparations for his dabbling in curses. The farmer did as he was instructed, and for many years his chapel could be seen along Highway 57. It is not known how effective his plan was or if the pig men continued to plague his every move. Legend states that eventually the chapel was moved to the sacred ground of a nearby cemetery. One chapel that certainly matches the description of the legend is the Saint Ghislane Chapel near St. Michael's Cemetery. No one except the farmer and the pig

The pig men of Brussels.

CASE 21 – THE PIG MEN OF BRUSSELS

men know for sure whether this is the exact chapel from the legend, but it may provide you with protection all the same.

As I mentioned, I first learned of this case through my good friend and colleague Linda Godfrey, who had dug up the old case for her book, *Strange Wisconsin*. Little else is known of the legend, including whether these strange pig men were ever spotted again. I investigated the old chapel and town of Brussels with fellow legend trippers Noah Voss, Sean Bindley, and Kevin Nelson. We inquired around about the legends, but no one was able to offer up any recent sightings of the odd creatures. Were the pig men merely a manifestation created by the fear and anger of the farmer, or did the botched curse truly backfire on him? Perhaps similar legends of this ilk would be better placed in a book on Wisconsin folklore, but the sheer strangeness of these creatures makes it impossible to me to leave them out of this guide. I truly don't know if these pig men are still roaming the countryside of Brussels, but it may serve you well to pop into the chapel for a quick prayer…just in case.

The Cumberland Beast

Where To Encounter It:

Wooded areas and back roads
Cumberland, WI

Directions:

The best bet for sightings of Bigfoot is to scour the wooded areas and back roads surrounding Cumberland.

CASE 22 – THE CUMBERLAND BEAST

Creature Lore:

One of the Native American beliefs is that these Sasquatch creatures are actually former shaman who used their powers to summon the dark arts and were punished by being condemned to spend eternity as these hideous creatures. These banished medicine men were turned into cannibalistic giants that were thought to possess supernatural powers and were to be avoided at all costs. According to Salish legend, a human may go crazy, pass out, or even lose their soul by the magic of a Sasquatch.

History of Lore:

Oral history of the local Native Americans tell of these giant bipeds freely roaming the land before modern development. I spoke with several elder tribesmen of the St. Croix Tribe, where stories of Sasquatch creatures have been passed down through the generations. One elder, Louis Bearheart, told me of a 55-year-old story from his childhood, when tribal members were startled by a Bigfoot creature that the tribe called a "screeching demon." Bravely, several of the tribeswomen gathered up their brooms and began swatting at the demon as they chased it back deep into the forest.

A Bigfoot carving that rests outside of a downtown Cumberland business.

WISCONSIN ROAD GUIDE TO MYSTERIOUS CREATURES

Over the past few decades reports of the bipedal beasts have popped up throughout the area, causing the tribal elders to perform a cleansing ceremony in order to ward off the unwelcome visitors. Several elders refused to speak about these creatures, citing their belief that these beings possess supernatural powers, and the mere mention of their existence will doom the storyteller with bad luck until they die.

Investigation Log:

One group that wholeheartedly believes in the Bigfoot curse is Loretta Potter and her family, who in 2002 were living in a home on the St. Croix Indian Reservation. Early on the morning of July 18, Loretta's son Peter was walking out to his car when a putrid stench caught his attention. He described the smell, saying, "It was rotten, like something dead." As he walked on he came within view of some creature that was both large and dark. Peter dashed back into his home to retrieve a flashlight so he could better identify the mysterious being. He returned outside just in time to hear the crunching of breaking braches as the creature fled into the woods. Peter stated that he felt the creature was more afraid of him than he was of it.

A few hours later, Loretta would have her own terrifying experience with the unknown biped. It was around 5am when Loretta awoke and headed to her kitchen to start some coffee. From her back kitchen window she noticed a dark figure pushed up against her daughter's window. That evening her daughter had invited a few friends over for a slumber party which made Loretta think that the being was some type of Peeping Tom. Panicking, Loretta moved in for a closer look and was shocked to discover a large, thin, hairy beast lurking outside the window. Loretta described the creature as being around 7-8 feet and noticed that it body was covered in

CASE 22 – THE CUMBERLAND BEAST

matted down hair. Strangely, the image reminded her of one of the apes from Tim Burton's *Planet of the Apes* movie, expect that the being's hairless grayish face appeared eerily human. At this point Loretta's olfactory sense was overwhelmed from a strong odor that she could only compare to rotting onions. Perhaps sensing Loretta's fear, the creature darted away from house at such a speed that Loretta claimed that she could barely see his movement. The next morning the family contacted the Barron County authorities along with the St. Croix Tribal Police, which sent out Officer Marvin Halverson. He reported to the scene and snapped some photos several footprints that he been left in the driveway. The prints were from some large creature with human-like toes. It was also in the safety of the daylight that the family noticed that, during the night, two of their pet rabbits had mysteriously disappeared.

A large footprint that was discovered outside the Potter home.

The Potter family was so disturbed by their Bigfoot sighting that Loretta took her family to the safety of a nearby hotel, where they spent an entire week recovering from their intense sightings. For a while the family tried to forget their Bigfoot encounters, yet the family believed that the Bigfoot curse had already attached. Soon after his Bigfoot encounter, Peter found himself without a job, crashed his car, and attended a party on the reservation when tragedy struck. Peter went to sit down on a chair and noticed that a gun was there. He went to move the gun, and it accidently went off, sending a stray bullet into the head of a young mother who was walking down the stairs, killing her. Eventually Loretta and her family moved from the house, hoping to put their Bigfoot experiences far behind them.

Strange activity in the area did not just center on the Potter family, as evidenced by the report we received from the neighbors who lived across the road from the Potter family. One evening between the hours of 12:30 and 3am, the homeowners were awoken by the sounds of something unknown scratching on the back of their home. The next morning the family was a bit puzzled over the scratching noise and decided to take a look around the house. When we investigated the case, we discovered a series of deep scratch marks etched into the home's siding approximately five feet above the ground. The family said that during their search around the perimeter of the home they had discovered large footprints as well. Unfortunately, it had rained the day before our investigation, washing away any possible evidence. What really troubled the family was the disappearance of six newborn puppies that went missing near the sweat lodge behind the house where other large footprints were seen. For the next few months we received several calls from others in the area reporting strange growling noises along with large unknown footprints.

Deep scratch marks were found carved into the siding of the house.

CASE 22 – THE CUMBERLAND BEAST

In 2003, the Outdoor Life Channel's show *Mysterious Encounters* taped an episode on the Cumberland Beast where they investigated many of the sightings of the mysterious creature. Although the show did not uncover any new evidence, it did bring national attention to the legend.

I recently spoke with a woman who lives in the area who remembered a bizarre encounter with a mysterious creature near Cumberland from 15 years ago. It was 7:30am as the woman braved the winter freeze and headed off to pick up a couple of her co-workers before going into the office. The woman was driving along on Highway G outside of Cumberland when she noticed something large standing near a creek in a steeply deep ravine 75 feet from the road. At first the woman thought it was nothing more than a bush, yet she wondered how she had never seen it before. As she slowed down she saw something large "standing straight up" by the creek. The motionless creature was estimated to be between 7-8 feet in height and was white in color. After picking up her friend, the two passed by the site again and, amazingly, the "thing" was still there. The friend also noticed the size of the figure, but neither of them could make out any fine details. What the two women agreed upon was that, whatever it was, it was tall and white. Unfortunately, the witness was unable to recognize any further specific physical characteristics of the beast. When the women returned from work later that afternoon, the creature was gone. The woman was truly puzzled by what she had seen and could not figure out what exactly it was. I talked with another of her co-workers, who said that she was the type of woman that "would not be prone to believing anything out of the ordinary," yet the story she told me was anything but ordinary.

WISCONSIN ROAD GUIDE TO MYSTERIOUS CREATURES

The Bigfoot of Granton

Where To Encounter It:

County Highway H
Granton, WI

Directions:

From downtown Granton, head north on County Road K. Follow K for a few miles and turn left (west) on County Road H. The sighting took place approximately 1 mile west of the K&H intersection, 100 feet east of the creek.

CASE 23 – THE BIGFOOT OF GRANTON

Creature Lore:

In the United States alone, hundreds of people report encountering a large unidentified hairy Bigfoot-like creature. For years, researchers have struggled with putting together a definitive profile of the beast's habits and lifestyles. When it comes to the actions of these creatures, witness accounts vary tremendously. Based on these sightings, Bigfoot creatures seem to have no real set patterns, leaving many questions unanswered. Are they nocturnal? Do they hibernate? What are their mating practices? What do they eat? Are they hostile? Are they supernatural? Do they live in packs? Etc… With so much uncertainty surrounding these giant creatures, we are left to speculate on their lifestyles based on the limited information we can garner from these sightings.

History of Lore:

Like many rural areas, the people living in the countryside of Clark County enjoy a slower and simpler pace of life. The beautiful rolling hills are offset by huge sections of heavily wooded forests. Numerous small creeks and brooks cut paths across the land, and travelers are treated to a showcase of old farmhouses and Amish farms that dot the ever-changing landscape. With plenty of game, water, and shelter, Clark County provides the perfect habitat for a large bipedal creature. The problem with collecting reports of the unusual is that small farming communities have traditionally been places where people refrain from expressing anything that would seem out of place with the flow, and Bigfoot sightings certainly would qualify as out of the ordinary. Perhaps this is the reason why no prior Bigfoot reports have surfaced from the area. Other research suggests that Bigfoot creatures are migratory creatures, continuously moving through established travel routes across

WISCONSIN ROAD GUIDE TO MYSTERIOUS CREATURES

the country. This, too, would account for the lack of reported sightings.

Investigation Log:

In 2000, James Hughes lived a quiet life in the countryside of Granton. Hughes, a part-time farmer, also delivered newspapers for the *Clark County Press*. The newspaper delivery required that he travel the back roads in the early morning hours. The route was unusually uneventful, but the early hours provided Hughes with an opportunity to welcome in the new day. This peacefulness of the country route all changed on the morning of March 28. Mr. Hughes was driving along CTH H, just a mile from his home, when he noticed something very big cross the road. He was able to gain a good look at the unknown creature before he headed back to his house to share the sighting with his wife. Not sure that anyone would believe him, Hughes debated whether he should report the incident. The next day Hughes called the Clark County Sheriff's Department. The department sent out Deputy Greg Herrick who interviewed Hughes. Here is the official interview from Deputy Herrick:

James Hughes stands at the spot of his Bigfoot encounter.

332: Jim, this is a voluntary statement on your behalf, do you understand that?

JH: Yup.

CASE 23 – THE BIGFOOT OF GRANTON

332: You called in a complaint into the sheriff's department for me on a object that you seen yesterday morning about 5:15 a.m., you describe it as 'Big Foot,' start from the beginning, on what, where you went yesterday morning, what you saw and what you were doing.

JH: Wife and I got up about 4 o'clock in the morning, shortly before 4, drank a cup of coffee, about quarter after I headed to Neillsville to pick up papers at Clark County Press. I got there right around 4:30, 25 to 5. It took me about 15 minutes, I talked to Dee maybe a minute or two, stopped at Kwik Trip, got a gallon of milk, three loaves of bread, pack of cigarettes, and headed home. So, I left Neillsville probably right around 5 o'clock. Pretty close to that, I never did check the watch. About a mile and a half from home, I broke over a hill and I seen something in the road, it was, he was, it was daylight enough, you could see without lights, but the clear was still (inaudible) on lights. There were no cars in sight, I seen there was something in the road, it was tall, but not very wide, it seemed like it moved to one side, I got no idea what the hell it was, as I got closer it, he, looked like a, like a real big big man. So, I got right near, right near a bridge and the lights, I had my lights on, I started slowly down, I didn't know what the hell it was, and the thing stepped off the road and it was on the edge of the road and it stepped in the ditch like it went one giant step and as I went by it was some kind of hairy critter, it must have been at least 8 feet high. I mean this thing was huge. It was all covered with a, it looked like a real dark grayish covered hair. The damn thing had something in its hand and it turned and looked at me as I went by, it resembled a face of an ape. And as I went by, the thing looked at me and I got scared as hell, I put my foot on the accelerator and left and got the hell out of there. When I walked through the door, I told my wife I wish to hell you went with me, and she says why and I says I think I see that goddamn 'Big Foot' and she says see, I told you they exist, I says goddamn, I never believed until now.

332: Starting back here you crossed this bridge and I'm looking in the Plat book, this bridge were talking about, it's going to be Panther Creek just west of H and K.

JH: I was looking at it enough that I ran off the road on the other side of the road.

332: You were eastbound?

JH: I was in east, yeah and I felt my tire leave the pavement and I jerked it back and just about that time I was going right past this critter where it was, the damn thing turned and I, I stepped on her and to hell to do and I didn't see no more and I didn't wait to find out, I got the hell out of there.

332: How tall did you think it was?

JH: Judging by the lay of the road, and sitting here right now, I'd say that damn thing was at least 8 feet high. At least.

332: About how wide at the shoulders?

JH: God, I don't, I don't know, it was huge, that's all I know.

332: How big do you think?

JH: Twice as wide as I am. I don't know. Three times maybe. I don't know.

332: How much do you think it weighed?

JH: I betcha the thing weighed 500 pounds.

332: Was it standing on 4 legs or 2?

JH: It was standing on 2 legs. It looked like a, like a king-size gorilla. I mean a huge bastard. That's what it looked like. He

CASE 23 – THE BIGFOOT OF GRANTON

was all hair, the arms, legs, head, everything was all hair. It was a dark grayish color from what I could make out. And he had something in its hand, it would have been the right hand like it might had been a carcass of a goat or something, I don't know. I didn't pay, really get a good look and I didn't want to wait around to find out. I seen that I got the hell out of here.

332: Were you scared?

JH: You're damn right I was scared. I was shitting right in my drawers; I got to tell you, all that's to it.

332: Were there any other vehicles in the area?

JH: Not that I know of, not that I remember.

332: Ever seen anything like this before?

JH: Never in my life. Not even a picture of in my life.

332: Just for a, I asked you this before, you know, imagine complaints like this are very rare, but no doubt there was probably something that you seen, but just for the record, you know, people are going to question it naturally and you feel the same way, are you on any medication?

JH: No I'm not.

332: Were you drinking at all?

JH: Nope.

332: Any drugs?

JH: No, I don't take, use drugs of any kind.

332: You're in good mental health?

JH: As far as I know, you may say different I don't know.

332: No.

JH: I know he is.

332: No, you're not doctoring with anybody?

JH: No. I'm perfectly fine, except for a bad back; I'm perfectly fine. And I put off calling, calling for, I was going to call yesterday, but I didn't call because people are going to think I'm nuts. I'm still afraid of it, but I was talked into calling this morning.

332: Um, okay keep us posted, if something else, if you hear anybody in the neighborhood talking or hear anything you let us know.

JH: I will.

332: Do you have anything else to add?

JH: No, I guess not, I just wished to Christ I knew what it was.

332: This will conclude interview with James, time is 11:10 a.m.

After conducting the interview, Deputy Herrick checked both the ditch area and plowed field for any signs of the creature. No tracks, feces, hair, or other evidence was obtained by the deputy during his search. To conclude the investigation, Clark County Sheriff Dale Olson wrote, "At this time the Clark County Sheriff's Department does not feel further investigation is needed. No further sightings have been reported. From information gathered it does not appear this creature is a threat to anyone."

Soon after the Bigfoot sighting I headed to Granton to interview Mr. Hughes for myself. Mr. Hughes was gracious enough to re-trace the event with me in order that I could see the exact spot where the creature was sighted. To me, one of the most intriguing aspects of the case was the goat or small animal that was being carried by the Bigfoot. Hughes told me that it looked like a goat, but he couldn't be sure as to what type of animal it was carrying. He was so terrified by the creature's deadly looking eyes that he didn't get a great look

CASE 23 – THE BIGFOOT OF GRANTON

at what was in its hand. Hughes stated that the creature's eyes were so threatening that he had trouble averting his gaze, which was the reason why he almost swerved off the road.

The terrain where the Bigfoot was sighted.

At first glance, it might be safe to assume that the Bigfoot had tracked and killed its prey. However, we need to keep in mind that it is entirely possible that it was not a goat the Bigfoot was carrying. Maybe it was a small deer, sheep or some other type of roadkill. Again, the speculative nature of the topic prohibits us from making any substantive claims. Not too far from where Hughes spotted the Bigfoot, I discovered that a gentleman was raising sheep on his farm. I inquired about any missing animals, but the farmer assured me that all of his livestock were accounted for.

A nearby farmer stated that none of his livestock were missing.

After spending the afternoon with Mr. Hughes, I was left with the impression that he was a down-to-earth, honest, and forthright man. It was my opinion that he was convinced that he had seen some type of unknown creature. He didn't seem prone to fanciful thinking and certainly didn't appear to be trying to hoax anyone. He told me that the reason he waited a day to report his sighting was because he feared that he would be ridiculed by his friends and neighbors. Yet, once the story broke, he was surprised to find that many of his neighbors told him that over the years, they too had seen some type of strange animal roaming the area.

In the lead-up of this book, I decided to revisit the case and travel back Granton to interview Mr. Hughes. I was very curious to hear what Mr. Hughes thought of his Bigfoot sighting now that over 10 years had passed, providing him plenty of time to reflect on the strange event. Unfortunately, upon arriving in Granton, I discovered

CASE 23 – THE BIGFOOT OF GRANTON

that he had passed away during the summer of 2009. Luckily, the new owner of his home also happened to be a friend of Mr. Hughes. He told me that over the years Hughes would often bring up his strange sighting, and right up to the day he died, he was absolutely certain that he had come face to face with a real Bigfoot.

WISCONSIN ROAD GUIDE TO MYSTERIOUS CREATURES

The Bigfoot of Danbury

Where To Encounter It:

Forests and back roads

Danbury, WI

Directions:

Most of the sightings have occurred in wooded areas and the back roads surrounding Danbury. The St. Croix State Forest is another hotbed for sightings.

CASE 24 – THE BIGFOOT OF DANBURY

Creature Lore:

The most widely-known and evasive creature in North America is one that goes by many names throughout the world. In Canada, the natives refer to it as a Sasquatch (wild man of the woods), in Australia locals call it the Yowie, the Chinese know it as the Yeti, yet when it is sighted in the Himalayan regions of India, Nepal, and Tibet, it is deemed the Abominable Snowman. Brazilians often spot the Mapinguary, in the Cascades locals call it Seeahtiks, and Argentineans have come face to face with the Ucumar. In the United States, the creature is best known simply as Bigfoot, and while the name of the creature varies widely, the appearance of these creatures is eerily similar. Based on thousands of first-hand eyewitness accounts, a general outline of their physical appearance has emerged. First, the creatures are extremely tall, their height ranging from seven feet all the way up to over 10 feet. Their mass is also considerable, as many reports estimate the weight of the creatures as being between 300-900 pounds. With such sheer girth, the creature also leaves unusually large footprints behind that have ranged from 12-24 inches in length and varied from 7-9 inches in width. Perhaps most unsettling is the fact that the creature is almost always described as a biped by those witnesses who have seen it walk and run on its hind legs. The beast is most commonly covered in long, thick, matted down, reddish-brown, auburn or black hair, although reports of beige, white, or silver colored hair have been filed. The creature's massive, intimidating body is heavily muscled with extremely broad shoulders. The lack of a neck, flat face and nose, sloped forehead, and pronounced eyebrow ridges only add to the unsettling appearance of the Bigfoot.

History of Lore:

The unincorporated community of Danbury budges right up to the Minnesota border along Wisconsin's northwest corner. With the 34,000-acre Saint Croix State Forest directly in Danbury's backyard, the area provides plenty of space for a large biped to roam unnoticed. Weird tales of Bigfoot creatures roaming the area date back many generations. The Native Americans of the area widely believed that the land was inhabited by these large elusive creatures. The nearby Ojibwe band of Indians refer to the creature as Bug-way'-jinini (wild man), and their oral history tells of the animal being around for quite some time.

Investigation Log:

For over three decades, Dennis Murphy has been researching and tracking the elusive Bigfoot through the northwoods of Wisconsin. It all started nearly 35 years ago when Murphy was scouting out a fishing spot north of Danbury. An avid outdoorsman, Murphy was in the secluded area when he came face to face with two large white-haired Bigfoot creatures. He caught a glimpse of the two Bigfoot creatures moving through the brush and noticed that they appeared very old, and one of them was over 9 feet tall. He noted that there was a substantial size difference between the two creatures. One was the size of a typical Bigfoot (7-9 feet tall), with large square shoulders. However, the second creature was considerably smaller than the first one, leading Murphy to the conclusion that it was either a female Bigfoot or possibly a young offspring. The multiple creatures sighted and the size difference make Murphy's sighting extremely fascinating, as the majority of Bigfoot sightings only involve one creature. The addition of a smaller possible female or young Bigfoot is also somewhat of a rarity. Fearing ridicule,

CASE 24 – THE BIGFOOT OF DANBURY

Murphy kept his strange sighting to himself. The experience was so bizarre that it sparked his life-long interest in Bigfoot, and that has lead to several additional sightings.

On June 1, 2002 while out searching for Bigfoot activity in Danbury, Murphy had another encounter with something unseen. Murphy stated that he could feel something following him as he heard a sound similar to that of a horse whinnying coming from nearby. He stealthily scanned the woods for the creature. As he listened, he heard something rustling in the distance. When he saw several high tree branches break off, he grabbed his camera and snapped some photos of the general area. Later, after getting the film developed, he believes he captured the outline of the Bigfoot creature (the photo is shown above in the title of this case). Adding to his evidence, Murphy discovered several large 17-inch footprints and was able to make a plaster cast of the mysterious print. To aid him on his investigations, Murphy commonly uses bait—he prefers using apples along with a few bananas. He also pointed out that he believes that the creatures are shy, mostly nocturnal, and are masters at avoiding humans.

Not all Danbury Bigfoot sightings come from those seeking out the creature. I received the following report from a gentleman whose

Dennis Murphy encountered this Bigfoot creature just north of Danbury.

gambling trip to Danbury took an unexpected turn toward the strange. He wrote:

> One summer night back in 2001, I drove a friend and his wife to a casino near Danbury, WI, for a night of gambling. On the way back home it started to rain pretty heavily so the driving was slow on the curvy roads of the northwoods. At one point I came over a hill and then was slightly startled when I heard my friend's wife scream, "What the heck is that?!" I looked over to the side of the road and saw a large creature with long swinging arms leap into the thick of the woods off the side of the road. I slowed a bit, waiting to see if the unknown creature would return, but it did not. We were all fairly excited and discussed what we had seen all the way home. I told some people at work and was laughed and scoffed at for a bit and then I didn't think about it for awhile. A month later I was visiting my father and he showed me the local paper which discussed a man who had seen a "Bigfoot" creature outside of Danbury years ago and has been searching for it ever since.

Dennis Murphy with a plaster cast of the Bigfoot's footprint.

CASE 25 – BLUE HILLS BIGFOOT

The Blue Hills Bigfoot

Where To Encounter It:

The Blue Hills Nature Area of Wisconsin, which is surrounded by the communities of Rice Lake, Ladysmith, Bruce, and Weyerhaeuser.

Directions:

Your best bet of encountering the Bigfoot creature is to hike any of the trails located inside the nature area. Surrounding woods also provide an excellent opportunity to encounter the creature...just make sure that all the land is public property.

WISCONSIN ROAD GUIDE TO MYSTERIOUS CREATURES

Creature Lore:

When most people think of Bigfoot, images of California, Washington, and Oregon forests spring to mind. Yet in the heart of Wisconsin's Blue Hills State Nature Area, a large hairy creature lurks. Reports of a giant biped inside the dense forest area have been circulating for many generations. Mysterious large footprints have also been discovered and are usually accompanied by a strange whistling call from a passing creature.

History of Lore:

The area of Rusk County has a long and sorted past when dealing with strange reports. In 1899, a "wild man" was captured in Rusk County. Newspaper accounts reported that while the creature was believed to be human, it had "lost nearly all semblance to a human being." The "man" was described as having long knotted hair and an equally lengthy unruly beard. He was clad only in torn up overalls, a filthy gunny sack, and an old coonskin hat. If seen in the wild, this man certainly would have cast an ominous presence and may have sparked some of the early legends of the Bigfoot creature of Rusk County. The identity of this wild man was never discovered, although authorities stated that "from appearances he has lived the life of a hermit in the wilderness for many years." According to the papers of the time, the man was simply shipped off to the insane asylum. What became of this wild man is unknown, and it seems the story was almost completely lost to history.

Investigation Log:

One of the most important aspects of investigating unknown creatures is to have a good understanding of the terrain in which they are alleged to inhabit. The Blue Hills Felsenmer State Natural

CASE 25 – BLUE HILLS BIGFOOT

Area is a solidly forested park in Rusk County. The Blue Hills area flows over into several rural communities and provides plenty of undisturbed territory for a cryptid to wander. With miles and miles of hiking trails through thick forest and brush, the place also provides limitless room for any legend hunter to explore.

An alleged Bigfoot nest in the heart of a Rice Lake forest.

In 1997, reports of a large, hairy Bigfoot creature caught the attention of both the media and researchers. On the 3rd of November, Brad Mortenson of the U.S. Expedition and Exploration Society discovered three large unknown tracks near Christy Mountain Ski Area. The tracks didn't match any known local animal. Mortenson told the *Rice Lake Chronotype* that the tracks "could be from the mysterious – some say mythical – ape like creature known as Bigfoot." At 16 to 17.5 inches long and 8 inches wide, it was the unusual dimensions of the tracks that made them stand out. Based on the placement of the tracks the gait of the creature was determined to be approximately 4 ½ feet. The Christie Mountain downhill ski area is a popular winter destination for skiers and snowboarders alike. Ironically, the company's mascot is a Bigfoot-like creature dubbed the "Blue Hills Beast." The mascot is dressed in a bright blue cookie monster-looking outfit that makes any misidentification of the mascot for Bigfoot highly unlikely.

The media coverage of the unknown tracks spurred others to come forward with their mysterious encounters inside the Blue Hills. However, these new witnesses weren't just discovering tracks; during his investigation, Mortenson even collected several firsthand eyewitness accounts of the hairy biped, including one from a woman who had a strange encounter with the beast while driving in the area. One evening while out driving, the woman caught sight of a large hairy Bigfoot creature crossing the road on its hind legs. The startled woman quickly noticed the creature's immense size, stating that the creature was much taller than her van, and she was equally amazed that it had such a fast pace, crossing the road in only two or three giant steps. The entire sighting happened so fast that the woman claimed that the creature had just appeared in her headlights and then was gone in a flash.

CASE 25 – BLUE HILLS BIGFOOT

The inside of the alleged Bigfoot nest.

In July of 1999, two hikers ventured off into the Blue Hills to explore the pristine forest. The two were walking along an old dirt road and enjoying the dense woods that surrounded them. The day was bright, peaceful and quiet, and as far as the hikers could tell, there wasn't another soul in sight. However, their tranquil hike was soon interrupted by a strange whistling sound coming from deep in the woods. The hikers were immediately struck by the oddness of the whistle, which they reported sounded more like some type of unusual call than just an ordinary whistle. With their ears perked up, the duo could not make out any other noises outside of the mysterious whistle vocalization. After listening to several more eerie whistles, their intuition told them that something was not quite right. Frightened, the hikers simultaneously sped off back toward their vehicle. Once back at the car, the two thought how uncharacteristic it was for them to be so easily scared. It wasn't until a few days later when they discovered that the whistle sound they heard matched other alleged Bigfoot calls that they decided to report the experiences to a Bigfoot website.

In the summer of 1999, while driving along Highway 53 just north of Rice Lake, the passenger of a car was leisurely gazing out the window and looked over to at a hill and spotted a large Bigfoot creature. The being was briskly walking up a hill that was covered with tall grass. A bit hesitant to come forward, the witnesses only spoke of the incident to close friends. It wasn't until other reports of the creatures began to surface that the witness decided to come forward with the encounter.

Talking with many locals, I gathered up several other puzzling sightings of something that resembled a large Bigfoot roaming the countryside of Rusk County. What adds intrigue to the stories is the complete randomness of the sightings. It seems that there is absolutely no rhyme or reason to any of the encounters. They mysterious events have taken place both during the day and night, and vary throughout several places within the county. Either the creature has a large and extensive roaming area, or perhaps we are dealing with multiple creatures all inhabiting the same general area.

CASE 26 – THE MINERAL POINT VAMPIRE

The Mineral Point Vampire

Where To Encounter It:

Graceland Cemetery
Fair Street
Mineral Point, WI

Directions:

From the south on Highway 151 take the Ridge St. exit and follow Ridge Street into town. Turn left on Fair Street; the cemetery will be on your left side.

Creature Lore:

Stories of blood thirsty creatures of the night have terrified cultures long into recorded history. Thanks to Hollywood, and a few popular book series, vampires are all the rage in today's popular culture. Modern portrayals of vampires have formed them into gorgeous models who freely roam the upper echelon of high society. Although these emotionally sensitive aristocratic super-humans need blood to survive, they have conveniently discovered a never-ending supply of human hosts willing to become their victims in exchange for an eternal life of ecstasy. Yet, vampires were not always cast in such a positive light. In fact, early descriptions of these nightwalkers describe them as hideous mindless ghouls who were hell bent on consuming the blood and flesh of humans. Early vampires did not even possess the ability to communicate and were universally viewed as undead beasts. They reeked of foul, rotting flesh and had rancid breath. Vampires of Eastern Europe were also clad in tattered rags, which were the dirt smeared remnants of their final burial outfit.

I actually spent several weeks in Romania traveling through Transylvania, searching for vampires and vampire lore. I scoured the countryside, digging up beliefs and legends of the feared monsters. During my expedition, I discovered countless unique customs and rituals which the villagers conducted in order to stop their deceased loved ones from transforming into these feared monsters. Locals believed that numerous measures had to be taken to ensure the eternal rest of their friends and family, including burying the body facing down, stuffing the mouth of the body with a rock or garlic, and making sure the body was buried on the other side of running water. If someone was extremely fearful of the dead coming back, they would drive a

CASE 26 – THE MINERAL POINT VAMPIRE

stake through the heart of the corpse or even decapitate the body and bury the head separate from the body. On my adventure, I even heard of a couple rare cases where the fear was so great that the community would cremate the deceased—grinding the cremated remains into a fine powder to make a soup that the whole community would consume, thereby spreading out the power of the dead spirit and preventing them from returning from the grave. Unfortunately, by the end of my expedition I had failed to spot any vampires in Transylvania…little did I know that if I wanted to spot a vampire, I could have stayed right here in my own home state of Wisconsin.

History of Lore:

Mineral Point is a small rural community tucked into the rolling hills of southwest Wisconsin. The quiet, charming little community is overflowing with history. Although the origins of the town date all the way back to 1827-1828, it wouldn't be until much later that the town made international headlines for being the home to numerous vampire sightings.

Investigation Log:

Mineral Point's official Vampire troubles began back on Monday, March 30, 1981, when Officer Jon Pepper was out on night patrol. The *Lethbridge Herald* reported, "Pepper was routinely shining his light through Graceland Cemetery when he saw 'a huge person with a white-painted face' wearing a dark cape." Officer Pepper quickly exited the car and chased the Dracula-looking creature across the sacred earth, but he finally gave up when the lighting fast creature somehow disappeared among the gravestones and flew over a cemetery fence.

WISCONSIN ROAD GUIDE TO MYSTERIOUS CREATURES

Mysterious vampire creature Officer Pepper chased through the cemetery.

Although it was in the dead of night, Officer Pepper was able to catch a decent glimpse of the thing as they raced through the graveyard. Pepper described the cloaked figure as being over 6 feet 3 inches in height, pale, thin, and very ugly. Pepper's weird description of the creature only served to make the case even more bizarre.

Back at his car, Officer Pepper tried to calm himself down from the unsuccessful capture of the trespasser. He was hesitant to make his report, as he knew how the story would sound. Regardless of the consequences, Pepper was on duty and felt that he had to file the report. Once Officer Pepper's report got out, media from all over the country descended upon the small town, looking for the Mineral Point Vampire. The publicity from the report generated a full-fledged vampire frenzy in town. Within hours of the news reports, dozens of additional sightings of the mysterious vampire poured in to the authorities, causing the *Wisconsin State Journal* to run the story "Vampires Stalk Mineral Point." The newspaper quoted Lt. Bill Trott as saying, "Last night (Tuesday) we had a half-dozen vampires on the loose in town." Lt. Trott continued his report, "We received several phone calls and were stopped by people on the street reporting encounters with white-faced creepy-looking people jumping out of

CASE 26 – THE MINERAL POINT VAMPIRE

the shadows at them." All of these separate accounts led to the theory that these sightings were not simply the work of one lone person or creature. Not surprisingly, the official police explanation had little to do with vampires, as they believed that the rash of subsequent sightings were the work of pranksters who took advantage of Officer Pepper's sighting and decided to cause some mischief of their own.

Cemetery fence that the vampire flew over to escape.

The police also purposed a more mundane explanation for Officer Pepper's sighting, theorizing that the mysterious intruder of the cemetery was not in fact a vampire, but was instead someone suffering from a mental illness. Perhaps, this explained the police department's hesitation to pursue the case further as the *Winnipeg Free Press,* picking up on the story, reported that the police were not eager to get back to the cemetery. "'I can't get anyone to go back to the cemetery at night,' Lt. William Trott said. 'I even offered to pay Pepper overtime to stake out the place for his vampire, but he wouldn't bite,' added the lawman with a chuckle." The unique phrasing chosen by Lt. Trott including "stake and bite" makes me wonder if he was having a bit of fun at the expense of the press. Even if Lt. Trott was being playful with the story, the *Wisconsin State Journal* reported that "Trott swears his report is not an April Fool's Joke."

With all the ambiguity surrounding this case, I decided to investigate the cemetery for myself. I set out with several investigators and we spent a couple dark nights patrolling the graveyard looking for any signs of a vampire residing in the area. While investigating this odd case in the daytime, we came across many life-long residents of Mineral Point who remembered the 1981 Vampire craze. What I found was that after all these years people still had a wide range of beliefs on the subject. Several residents told me that Officer Pepper was a trickster and prankster who loved to pull gags on his friends and family. Other stood up for the credibility of the sighting, stating that the original description was accurate. Still others whispered the stories of those who had also encountered similar unidentified creatures roaming the area of Graceland Cemetery.

For years we tried to track down Officer Pepper to get his take on the whole situation. According to the Mineral Point Police Department, they do not have any police records from 1981, which, of course, only enhances the mystery of the event. Local legends states that Officer Pepper was so plagued by all the unwanted attention his story had garnered that he quit the police force, moved away, and refused to speak of the event ever again. Well, like most legends, this one is partly true. Jon Pepper is now working for the Iowa County Sheriff's Department, and it seems he doesn't want to revisit the case, as my many requests for an interview or comment have disappeared into the night…just like the Vampire of 1981.

Author Bio

Chad Lewis – Is a researcher, author, and lecturer on topics of the strange and unusual. He has a Master of Science Degree in Psychology and has trekked across the world in search of the paranormal. From tracking vampires in Transylvania and chasing the Chupacabras in Puerto Rico, to searching for the elusive monster in Loch Ness, and pursuing ghosts in Ireland's castles, Chad brings over 16 years of research experience to his work.

Chad has been featured on the Discovery Channel's "A Haunting," ABC's "World's Scariest Places," and hundreds of radio interviews, TV appearances, and newspaper articles. Chad is also the author and co-author of numerous books on the strange and unusual.

To reach Chad, go to his websites:
www.unexplainedresearch.com or www.ontheroadpublications.com

You can also email him at chadlewis44@hotmail.com

Other Titles Authored/Co-Authored by Chad Lewis

Haunted Places

The Illinois Road Guide to Haunted Locations

The Iowa Road Guide to Haunted Locations

The Florida Road Guide to Haunted Locations

The Minnesota Road Guide to Haunted Locations

The South Dakota Road Guide to Haunted Locations

The Wisconsin Road Guide to Haunted Locations

Haunted St. Paul

Paranormal

Hidden Headlines of New York

Hidden Headlines of Texas

Hidden Headlines of Wisconsin

Gangsters

The Minnesota Road Guide to Gangster Hot Spots

The Wisconsin Road Guide to Gangster Hot Spots